FACES
AT THE
WINDOW

By Paul F. Eno

Published by
New River Press
645 Fairmount Street
Woonsocket, R.I.02895
(800) 244-1257
www.NewRiverPress.com

SECOND EDITION 2001

ISBN 1-891724-01-0

Cover Photo by Paul F. Eno

Printed in Canada

To my father,
from whom I learned not only love
but the love of all things mysterious.

Contents

Faces at the Window

Introduction

Objectivity has never been easy, but in the waning years of the 20th century, with their fads, political correctness and paranoia, it's darn near impossible. Given people's desperate need to believe in something beyond themselves, that's especially true with the phenomena we call "paranormal," phenomena that popular tradition has labeled supernatural: ghosts, poltergeists, vampires, mysterious animals, UFOs, etc.

Despite these difficulties, I've tried to be as objective as possible in dealing with the varied cases in this book, most of which I witnessed first-hand. I'm an open-minded skeptic, but all paranormal phenomena must be thoroughly sifted through the mesh of science and philosophy before they get any credence from me. The cases in this book are the most remarkable I encountered in my first years as a paranormal investigator/journalist, and they're the most difficult to explain. I retell them from my notes, vivid recollections (experiences like these aren't easy to forget) and previous writings.

Time and scientific discovery have changed many of the opinions I expressed as these cases occurred, however. Modern physics has virtually proven that we live in a world very different from what our senses tell us: a world in which time is an illusion and in which matter is just another form of energy. While many theoretical physicists breathe fire at this, I believe that the bold, pioneering science of quantum mechanics can do lots to explain much paranormal phenomena: moreso than religion, mysticism or superstition. With its interplay of pseudo-conscious subatomic particles that defy time and seem directly affected by human minds, quantum mechanics can, I feel, explain in one swat most instances of what we call ghosts, poltergeists, reincarnation experiences, clairvoyance, clairaudience and a mountain of others.

Some physicists agree. Many don't, but since I probably know at least as much about physics as they know about paranormal phenomena, I consider my opinion as valid as theirs. So we're almost certainly dealing with natural, not supernatural, phenomena, but the natural "laws" involved are far more bizarre than any classical supernatural explanation.

That's what I find so wonderful!

From the viewpoint of the paranormal, a critical theory in quantum mechanics is the notion of "multiple universes." According to this theory, which is backed up almost frighteningly by some equations and experiments with subatomic particles, there are an infinite number of universes existing side by side and through which our consciousnesses constantly pass. In these universes, all possibilities exist. You are alive in some, long dead in others, and never existed in still others. Many of our "ghosts" could indeed by visions of people going about their business in a parallel universe or another time — or both.

In one revealing case in the American Midwest, for example, a seance (a practice I discourage, by the way) revealed that the household "ghost" thought that the home's inhabitants were ghosts and were haunting him!

A mutual glimpse across parallel universes? It's more common than you may realize.

The more science discovers about nature, the more we see how utterly unified all life — and indeed all things — really are.... a point bitterly proven by the environmental crisis. It's plain to see, for example, that "Earth forces," especially electromagnetism, seem to affect both the human mind and paranormal phenomena. I've seen that seemingly unrelated factors, such as the interplay of geology, magnetism and water-table level actually can contribute their energies to paranormal phenomena in a given area.

But all that isn't enough to explain everything I've seen in my many years of "ghost hunting." I'm a journalist, not a scientist, but I'm not blind. It's impossible for me to escape the conclusion that there are life forms, extra-dimensional or extra-temporal in the sense of physics, that influence many paranormal situations. If they do exist, I believe they're natural, not supernatural, creatures. They're just from a part of nature we haven't visited yet. I believe they feed off people's psychic energy and create or contribute to many of the phenomena we call paranormal.

And why not? Life is infinitely varied, and its possibilities are endless. In such a world, the classical understanding of life, the ghost, the poltergeist and past-life/parallel-life experiences take on incredible new dimensions.

I hope this book does much more than titillate the curious, since I mean to convey, along with the facts and the possibilities, the poignancy and human suffering that so frequently accompany these phenomena. Fascinating or not, I hope that you and those you love never have to endure them.

Paul F. Eno
Town's End, 1998

Faces at the Window

Glossary

Apparition

—The visible form of an entity

Divination, divining

—An ancient practice that uses one or another instrument (including mirrors, pendula, ouija boards, dowsing rods, etc.) to learn information not available to the physical senses.

Ghost

—*Popular definition:* The spirit of a dead person or animal that has remained on Earth for one reason or another

—*More likely:* **a)** The "psychic residue" of a dead person's most traumatic experiences left in a place and "picked up" by an observer **b)** The experience of entities from one or more "parallel universes" as hypothesized in theoretical physics.

Poltergeist

From two German words meaning "noisy spirit."

—*Popular definition:* A mischievous ghost or evil spirit.

—*More likely:* The psychic byproduct of a troubled and frustrated human mind, usually that of a child about to go through puberty, a highly traumatic time. Phenomena can include destruction of property, physical assaults on the subject, apparitions, odors and noises.

Psi

—A catch-all term for human extrasensory communication with the environment and other people.

Psychical

— Referring to phenomena that cannot be explained or described in terms of established physical principles.

Psychic Photography

—A phenomenon in which ghostly streaks, faces, people or other attributes appear on photographic negatives or prints. Usually, the photographer is unaware of the "extras" in the photos until they are developed. Also refers to the conscious projection of mental images onto photographic film.

Psychokinesis (PK)

—Also called telekinesis. The influence of a human mind or minds on external objects or processes without the mediation of known physical forces.

Telepathy

—Extrasensory awareness of another person's mind. It's probable that all of us are in constant but unconscious contact with other people and the environment in this way.

Vampire

—*Popular definition:* An evil spirit possessing the body of a dead person and needing blood to keep the body alive.

—*More likely:* A living person who develops a pathological lust for blood or suffers from one or another now known diseases, none of them supernatural.

Faces at the Window

I

The Bridgeport Poltergeist

*An original version of this story appeared as "Beseiged by a Demon" in
the May and June 1985 issues of FATE magazine. Original elements are
used here by permission of Llewellyn Worldwide, Ltd.*

Faces at the Window

Before it became the home of one of the most publicized poltergeist hauntings of the 20th century, the house on Lindley Street in Bridgeport, Connecticut, was a place one would never notice. But for a few weeks in November 1974, it became an address known the world over as events there tied up an entire city for days.

A modest, one-storey bungalow, the house stands in a blue-collar neighborhood in the north end of one of New England's most depressed cities.

The house's history isn't especially unusual: Built about 1915 for the son of a local clothing manufacturer, it was at one time or another home port for a congressional candidate, a city park official and a few lesser-known denizens. In 1960, Gerard and Laura Goodin, a quiet couple who kept to themselves, moved in.

During their first years on Lindley Street, the Goodins gave birth to a young son who died in 1967. Overcome with grief, the couple, then in their 40s, decided to adopt a three year-old Canadian Indian girl named Marcia (pronounced Mar-SEE-a), a beautiful, black-haired tot who was intelligent, clever and imaginative. Acquaintances often noted the protectiveness with which her new parents surrounded Marcia.

In was in early 1972 that something started pounding on the walls of the house. In a 1975 radio interview, Goodin said the noises sounded at all hours and always had a pattern.

"The noises would begin as a tapping and then go into an awful bang," he said, adding that he often called his wife from the factory where he worked, sometimes hearing the noises in the background. Occasionally the tappings would be muted; at other times the house would shudder from the force of the blows.

Investigators later noted that construction of a new wing of nearby St. Vincent's Hospital was taking place during that time, but Goodin discounted the possibility that this

Faces at the Window

had anything to do with the noises. He did suspect that neighbors might be playing pranks, especially since the sounds seemed to increase around Halloween.

The Goodins confided their situation to one of their few friends in the neighborhood, John Holsworth, a patrolman on the Bridgeport Police Department, who lived across the street. Goodin and Holsworth recorded the sounds. The tape reveals rhythmic pounding, like that made by a fist hitting wood. The racket stopped about six weeks after the neighbors Goodin suspected moved away, bringing at least temporary peace.

But a few months later, the racket started again, and it was worse than ever. Fed up, the Goodins called on city officials for help. Their pleas brought police and fire department investigators as well as city engineers who, after a thorough check, pronounced the walls, foundation and plumbing sound and not responsible for the clamor. Nobody thought to attribute the sounds to anything other than natural causes.

The hullabaloo continued, despite all efforts to explain and stop it, on into 1974 and through that summer and fall. Sometimes it would stop for a week or two, then break out afresh.

Then things took a more frightening turn.

Wet footprints on a dry night

Late on a summer night that year, a disembodied hand reportedly appeared at a front window. In the early fall, Mrs. Goodin answered a triple knock at the front door, only to find a set of wet footprints on a perfectly dry night. At about 4:30 p.m. on Thursday, November 21, the family was eating an early dinner in the kitchen when the sound of smashing glass came from the front room. Running down the short hallway, Goodin found that the window to the left of the front door had been smashed *from the inside*. Only the three Goodins had been in the house. All remained quiet until about four o'clock the next afternoon, when the curtains in the front room suddenly fell off the wall.

The Goodins had the habit of driving to New York City, some 50 miles away, every second Saturday to relax and shop. November 23 happened to be their Saturday to go, and they left the house at about 8:30 a.m. When they returned at about 5 p.m., the Goodins were shocked to find that the portable television in Marcia's room, adjacent to the kitchen, had somehow moved from its shelf to her bed, where it lay face down. Goodin later told police that he had no sooner placed the television back on its shelf than dishes rose from the sink and started flying around the kitchen.

The Goodins, who were conservative Roman Catholics, kept traditional religious articles in each room. Many of these started to jump from the walls and crash to the floor. As soon as Goodin put them back where they belonged, most of them hurtled away again. Then the horrified family watched the 350-pound refrigerator rise about half a foot off the floor and saw the television console in the kitchen keel over.

That night, the house rocked with the worst poundings the family had ever endured. As Goodin later recalled, the sounds "went from wall to wall and room to room, then stopped about midnight."

"At 8 a.m. Sunday (November 24) I got up when I heard a racket in the next room. I went in and saw a table turn over. Then another table just lifted up and fell. Chairs just picked themselves up and started going every which way. And there was nobody in the room but me!" he told me later.

Help us!

Just before 8:30 a.m., the telephone rang at the home of Harold and Mary Hofmann, friends who lived eight blocks away.

"Help us!" shouted Laura Goodin in a shaking voice. "Strange things are happening!"

Faces at the Window

Hofmann quickly drove to the Lindley Street address and was stunned at what met his eyes. "The place was a mess," he later told a reporter. "Tables were overturned and knives, forks and dishes lay all over the floor. The big console TV was lying on its side. While I put it back in place, a small portable TV began rocking back and forth by itself. No one else was even in the room!"

Not long afterward, Holsworth was outside his house and noticed the Goodins on their porch. When they spotted him, they called and waved hysterically. The off-duty policeman sprinted across the street and entered the house, where he watched in consternation as the refrigerator lifted slowly off the floor, turned at right angles and then set down again.

"Then the big TV just seemed to float into the air and crash to the floor," he said later.

For several hours, everyone stood around frantically trying to understand what was happening. Holsworth searched high and low for wires and other devices that could cause such disturbances but found nothing.

"Things were going on in one room and then the next, as if whatever it was was moving from room to room," Goodin said. "The knife holder over the kitchen sink flew off the wall toward me. I caught it."

In the middle of this bizarre morning, Hofmann called Ed and Lorraine Warren in nearby Monroe. The Warrens, long famous as paranormal investigators and lecturers, promised to drive over to look into the situation. As far as I know, Hofmann knew the Warrens only by reputation.

Terrified policemen

Meanwhile, an exasperated Holsworth decided to call in some of his on-duty police comrades. Here's the report filed by Patrolman Joseph Tomek, one of the first to arrive:

> **TO: Captain Charles Baker**
> **FROM: Ptlm. Joseph Tomek**

Faces at the Window

REG: File #74-79962 - Suspicious Activity 24
November 1974
Sir: At 10:11 A.M. an R.C. G-35 was detailed to
. . . Lindley Street on a report of strange activity going on inside the house. . . . On arrival
Ptlm. Joseph Tomek and Carl Leonzi observed
the inside of the house in disarray: furniture,
pictures, religious articles, personal belongings,
etc., were thrown about in all rooms except one.
Mr. Garad [sic] Goodin, age 56, his wife Loura
[sic], age 50, and their adopted daughter
Marcia, age 10, were present ....

While conducting the initial investigation, Ptlm.
Joseph Tomek, Carl Leonzi, George Wilson and
Leroy Lawson observed one or more of the following happen: the refrigerator rise approximately six inches off the floor; a 21 inch portable TV set in the living room rise off a table
and turn around; furniture move away from the
wall and fall over; object [sic] on shelves and
hanging from the walls start vibrating .... Also
observed was a lounge chair that Marcia was
sitting in move rapidly backwards and overturn.
When Officers at the scene tried to move the
chair, they did so with great difficulty.

At this time the Bridgeport Fire Dept. was called
to the scene to inspect the building. Sgt.
Mangaiamele (Sector Sergeant) also was notified. Chief Zwierlien stated the building to be
structurally sound and could offer no physical
reason for what was happening. While the chief,
firemen and Sgt. Mangaiamele were at the
scene, they observed furniture and articles move
about and fall. Chief Zwierlien stated he believed witchcraft to be the cause.

Father Doyle from St. Patrick's Church was
called to the scene and stated he believed the
happenings to be caused by an unknown spiritual [sic] being. He gave a blessing on the house

Faces at the Window

and its occupants and stated he would make a few telephone calls and return later. About this time the strange events started to cease. An unidentified neighbor telephoned Mr. Edward Warren (sic)... who is a Physic (sic) Researcher, specializing in this kind of phenomenon. On his arrival he interviewed all parties that were involved. He stated he believed the events to be caused by a phenomenon being produced by Marcia called "poltergist [sic] activity." (That is that Marcia is able to make things happen by unconscious concentration.) At this time Mr. Warren telephoned Father William Charbonneau of St. John of the Cross Church in Middlebury, Conn . . . .

Father Charbonneau arrived at approximately 1:00 P.M. and conducted interviews with all persons who had observed any of the events. . . . He then blessed all parties that had observed anything . . . . All officers left the scene at approximately 2:45 P.M. All seemed quiet and normal . . . .

Entering the house that surreal morning, another policeman immediately saw "a picture fall off the wall, a small desk moved and the clock on the kitchen wall fell." He at once *backed* out of the house and waited in the patrol car for his partner!

Policemen and firemen that morning had not been told they would be going to a "haunted house," only that they were to investigate "suspicious activity." Patrolman Leonzi expressed the attitude of the city personnel who were there that morning when he said, "Everything was unreal. Everything was moving."

While all this was going on that Sunday morning, I was driving the 60 miles from my home in East Hartford to the Warrens' house in Monroe for what I expected to be a quiet dinner with my friends Ed and his wife, Lorraine, a well known psychic. The Warrens, who even then had over 20 years' experience dealing with the paranormal, had been advisers in my own research for several years. As for me, I was a 21 year-old seminary college student, with majors in philosophy and abnormal psychology, just home for Thanksgiving vacation. I didn't know it yet, but it was going to be a vacation I'd never forget. Were it not for the flat tire I suddenly had to change along the way, I might have missed meeting the Bridgeport poltergeist. As it was, I arrived at the Warren home at about 12:30 p.m., just as they were getting back from their morning in Bridgeport to meet Fr. Charbonneau and take him to Lindley Street for the visit recorded by officer Tomek.

"Paul, are you in a high spiritual state right now?" Lorraine asked in a worried voice as I breezed in. I knew what this question meant: There was a big case about to break, and the Warrens wanted me in on it.

Needless to say, I never got my dinner. Ed and I left for the Goodin home, while Lorraine and Fr. Charbonneau followed as soon as the priest arrived. On the way to Bridgeport, some 10 miles away, Ed told me about another incident that had just taken place: One of Mrs. Goodin's toes had been broken by a falling television set.

Why us?

When we turned into Lindley Street, the sight was unbelievable. The road was jammed with traffic, and a huge crowd had begun to gather in front of the house, on both sides of the street. Policemen were lined up in front of the tiny bungalow. Several officers escorted us inside, where chaos reigned. The place was packed with policemen, firemen and concerned neighbors. Clothing, furniture and oddments were strewn everywhere. Immediately after we arrived, Mrs. Goodin, complete with broken toe, returned from the emergency room at St. Vincent's Hospital.

As soon as the graying, heavy-set woman entered the

house, hobbling on a cane, Ed Warren introduced the priest and me. Mrs. Goodin at once grabbed my arm and pointed to a toy baby carriage parked near the living-room television. She said "the thing" had piled articles of Marcia's clothing and toys into it and then rolled it there.

"Why us?" she asked in a desperate voice.

Passing down the short hallway into the kitchen, Ed noticed that the bathroom was extremely cluttered. Throughout the rest of that day and Monday, objects were continually spilling and falling in the tiny bathroom, and the tub was constantly filled with a variety of objects.

The kitchen was worse. I found Goodin sitting at the kitchen table with his head in his hands. The stumpy, tired-looking man extended a hand without changing his expression of helpless resignation, "Have you ever seen anything like this in your life?" he asked.

I had to say no: I had never seen a poltergeist do quite this much damage. It looked as though invisible antagonists had been having a brawl there. Dishes were smashed all over the floor and there were only bare hooks on the wall where religious objects had hung. Much of the furniture was knocked over.

Marcy

Told I would find Marcy in the cellar, I descended the stairs and found her talking with two enormous policemen, one a sergeant. The girl was sitting on a stool in the corner, cuddling her orange and white cat, Sam. From the way the policemen were talking to her, it was clear that they either doubted her mental balance or suspected she had caused all the trouble.

After they left, I had a long talk with Marcy. Here, I learned, was an intense, introverted and imaginative child who said that the cat was her only friend. I discovered that she had been kept home from school for the previous six weeks because a boy there had kicked her and hurt her back,

Faces at the Window

although the injury was minor. I also noted that Marcy didn't seem frightened of what was going on. Obviously she was happy to accept the thick shell of protection her adoptive parents had thrown around her.

Gerard and Laura Goodin characterized Marcy as a normal, obedient and loving daughter with a vivid imagination and artistic talent. She gave visitors the same impression. But longtime family friends told stories of a much different Marcy Goodin: moody, deceitful and disrespectful.

"She does sneaky things when her mother's not around," one said, suggesting that parental overprotection was responsible. "Her mother never lets her go out to play. She's always in the house."

After a while, another policeman came into the cellar and prodded Marcy with questions about whether Sam the cat could really talk. The girl immediately pulled back into her shell. Apparently, the policemen just arriving at Lindley Street and who had seen nothing unusual were already trying to find a hoax and to pin it on Marcy.

The talking cat

Perhaps this is as good a time as any to deal with the question of the "talking cat," featured in more than a few headlines during the episode. It was perfectly clear to me that Marcy would occasionally hold the cat close to her and make sounds that may have seemed as if they were coming from the animal. The plucky feline had been in the veterinary hospital for an operation several months before. After he returned, the Goodins and even some of their neighbors insisted quite vehemently that the cat had begun to talk.

While at the clinic, Goodin told me, "the damn thing must have swallowed a myna bird." He swore that the cat would come to the top of the cellar stairs and demand in picturesque language to be let out. Sometimes he "swore like a sailor," I was told. At other times, according to Goodin, Sam would literally pound on the door and shout, "Open this door, you dirty Frenchman, you dirty rat!"

When I thrust my tongue deep into my cheek and suggested that perhaps Sam was possessed by the ghost of James Cagney, Goodin was not amused.

I spent the better part of three days watching Marcy, and I wasn't born yesterday. I saw nothing to indicate that Sam was anything but an ordinary cat with ordinary abilities. The media made much of him, though, and I will never forget the sight of reporters from the three major television networks standing around Sam with microphones that Monday, begging him to say something!

Fr. Charbonneau joined Marcy and me in the cellar at about 3:30 Sunday afternoon. He spoke with the girl for some time and noted the same characteristics I had. He said she told him she thought it was fun having so many people in the house, although she seemed to make no attempt to be the center of attention.

Meanwhile, the story of the Bridgeport poltergeist was spreading far and wide across the land. The crowd near the house had now reached 500 and was growing rapidly. Traffic in the area had come to a virtual standstill.

The police left the house at about 2:45 p.m., although a few remained outside to keep the crowd under control. Reporters began arriving at 4 p.m. and roamed freely through the house, talking with the Goodins, the Warrens and me. I decided to permit reporters to use only my first name. My position as a seminary student required a certain degree of anonymity: Some of my superiors looked askance at my involvement in psychical research, and publicity was the last thing I needed.

At 4 p.m. the Warrens, Fr. Charbonneau and I had the first of many conferences. With the exception of the priest, who had to return to his parish in the morning, we could remain on the case as long as necessary. We decided that I would stay with Marcy to watch and make sure she was not directly responsible for any of the events.

Faces at the Window

After that, we decided to return to Monroe for more discussion and something to eat. First, however, Fr. Charbonneau blessed the house, using a ritual similar to the one Fr. Doyle had used that morning. The Warrens accompanied the priest from room to room as he prayed and sprinkled holy water. I stayed in the living room with the family.

The flying dresser

As we were about to leave the house, we heard a crash coming from Marcy's bedroom. The big dresser had been thrown across the room, smashing into the closet door on the other side. Everyone was in the living room when it happened. This was our introduction to whatever it was that had brought us here. The crowd stared and whispered as we left the house. No doubt they had expected Father Charbonneau to come flying out a window as had happened in the then-new film *The Exorcist.*

Back at the Warrens' house, the three of us (Fr. Charbonneau had an appointment in Waterbury) tried to put things together. Although we had not seen or heard the most dramatic events, we had little doubt that we were dealing with a poltergeist. Since this phenomenon is little understood even today, many investigators have their own variations on the common theories. Ours were that either Marcy's pent-up psychic energy was responsible for the poltergeist or that one or more actual demonic entities were at work. Only time and the phenomena themselves would give us an answer.

The four of us returned to Lindley Street at about 8 p.m. that evening to find that the crowds had swelled to several thousand. The story was now out on the news wires of the Associated Press, United Press International and Reuters, as well as the major broadcast networks.

The spontaneous burn

An hour later, we were drinking coffee in the kitchen when Lorraine Warren suddenly cried out in pain. As we watched, a blister slowly appeared on the top of her left hand. The hand, in plain sight all the time, had certainly not come in contact with anything that could have caused such a burn. No one was smoking, either. Fearing the rare but terrifying phenomenon of "spontaneous human combustion," Ed tried to persuade his wife to leave the house. She refused.

An hour and a half later, Marcy was in her room showing Fr. Charbonneau a charm bracelet. Suddenly the big bureau, which had been set back in place against the wall, again flew across the room. No one was near it. The predominance of activity in this room was confirming what we suspected: Marcy's bedroom, and most likely Marcy herself, were the focal points of the phenomena.

Attacked by the television

Everyone gathered in the kitchen at about 11 p.m. I was standing next to the television console there, and Marcy was by my side when Goodin suddenly pointed to the TV. The flowers in a small vase on top of it were moving silently, as if fluttering in a breeze. Goodin said that whenever the flowers moved like that, the television was going to fall over.

I felt around the flowers with my fingertips. They were engulfed by the trademark "psychic cold" that no thermometer measures but that's all too familiar to every psychical researcher. I felt behind the television as far as I could reach. The strange cold was there too. Then, as I leaned against the sink, the TV went over with a crash, face down, hitting my left leg and knocking Marcy and me across the kitchen. Feeling the force of the crash, I was astonished that the television was undamaged. But my leg sported a minor gash for several weeks, a battle scar from my bout with the Bridgeport poltergeist.

Faces at the Window

After this, things quieted down. Later, at nearly 2 a.m., Fr. Charbonneau blessed the house again. If indeed the haunting was demonic in nature, we hoped this would end it without recourse to more drastic measures such as exorcism. Things remained calm for the rest of the night.

At 4 on the morning of Monday, November 25, we returned to Monroe to get some sleep. Fr. Charbonneau stretched out on the living-room couch, while Lorraine Warren and I lingered in the kitchen, drinking tea and talking. She had just said how much she hoped the Lindley Street incident was ended when we both felt a "presence." Whether connected with the Lindley Street case or not, something invisible, inaudible and malign was in the kitchen with us. Lorraine and I held hands across the table and prayed. Whatever it was soon left, but from then on she was as unsure as I that this poltergeist would be so quickly banished.

Worse than ever

At exactly 8 a.m., the telephone rang. Fr. Charbonneau had left to celebrate Mass at his parish, but the rest of us were asleep. Lorraine answered and heard our fears confirmed: Laura Goodin frantically reported that everything had started all over again, and that the destruction was worse than ever.

Back on Lindley Street, we found the interior of the house a shambles and the place jammed with police and reporters, including network journalists. Mrs. Goodin was wearing a crucifix on a black ribbon around her neck. After hearing a full report on the events of the early morning (which were similar to those of Sunday morning), we started tossing out the reporters and curiosity seekers who had wandered boldly into the house. It took until noon to get people sorted out and ejected. I was with Marcy during the entire period.

By this time we had all but decided that an exorcism of the house was the only course left. That wasn't as easy as it sounded. Unlike Protestants, Eastern Orthodox and Jews,

Faces at the Window

Roman Catholics have highly ritualized and "official" forms of exorcism. A Roman Catholic priest can find himself in big trouble with his bishop if he uses these rituals without permission, especially in a highly public situation.

That afternoon we tried to get some cooperation from the Roman Catholic Diocese of Bridgeport, to no avail. Msgr. John J. Toomey, vicar general of the diocese, later issued a written statement saying, among other things, that Church officials attributed the events to "purely natural causes," as though they were in any position to judge.

Fr. Charbonneau was in an awkward situation because he wasn't even from that diocese. In desperation, I called an Eastern Orthodox priest I knew and asked if he would be willing to come and pray an exorcism. He said yes, but only as a last resort since the Goodins should have recourse to their own Church first. Thus, as the day passed and pressure increased from both the family and the police to do something to end the nightmare, we found ourselves in the proverbial *Catch-22* situation.

Facing off with the entities

Around 1 p.m., I left the house and waded through the incredible crowd (which the media claimed was nearing 10,000) to go to a store and get some snacks for everyone. People in the crowd, evidently thinking I was "Fr. Bill" Charbonneau (who was only a few years older than I and was getting a good many headlines), either stared in awe or tried to ask questions, which I evaded. I bought candy for everyone and was back in the house by 1:30. The Warrens then left to talk with some reporters at their home.

This left the Goodins, Marcy's babysitter (a neighbor), *Bridgeport Post* reporter John Sopko and me in the house. Marcy, the babysitter and I began to play a board game while the others chatted. Suddenly an acrid smell, like ozone mixed with sulfur, drifted through the house. It came from the kitchen. Instantly, Goodin was up and dashed into the kitchen; he was in plain sight every moment.

"Oh, oh," he said. "It's going to start again!"

Our skin jumped with that unmistakable electrical tingle that's burned into the mind of anyone who has ever witnessed poltergeist phenomena close-up. A whitish, gauzy cloud began to form in the kitchen, and Goodin was back in the living room at once. I immediately sat everyone down and took out a prayer book I had with me, starting to chant the first thing I came upon. It happened to be an ancient "akathist" or hymn in praise of Jesus Christ. In a touching scene, Marcy came over and joined me in the simple hymn. Mrs. Goodin wept. The malign presence quickly dissipated.

The Warrens returned about 3:30 p.m. During the next few hours, as we waited vainly for a return call from the Bridgeport Diocese, we sat in the kitchen and listened to the radio. We were joined by two policemen. Practically every station to which we turned was talking about the house on Lindley Street. One officer rudely hinted that a hoax was the only explanation. His mockery ended when the kitchen was suddenly engulfed again with the smell of sulfur and ozone, this time coming from Marcy's room. But nothing further happened.

We sent out for food, then the Warrens left again to return home to make a number of long-distance phone calls to other paranormal investigators and influential clergymen. Only the Goodins and I were in the house at about 7:10 p.m., when I suddenly got the feeling that something was very wrong. Goodin felt it too and went into the kitchen. The cloudlike formation and the malign presence soon returned, now seeming much stronger. (Oddly, I had the clear impression that it was exactly four times stronger.)

Someone who has never experienced such a thing cannot imagine the certainty all of us felt at that moment that entities were "arriving." Although invisible, their movements were immediately obvious to us from moment to moment as they moved from the kitchen, down the short hallway

Faces at the Window

and into the living room. Goodin traced one as it did this. Mrs. Goodin started to cry, while Marcy clung to me in terror. I chanted the akathist prayer again.

Then, to the amazement of everyone, especially me, Goodin began chanting in a beautiful bass voice that I would have sworn was not his own, a prayer in flawless Latin that sounded to me like part of the old Roman Catholic Funeral Mass. He later said he had never studied Latin but remembered some of the language from his days as an altar boy. Well, I'd never heard of any altar boy who absorbed that much proper vocabulary and pronunciation just by kneeling at the foot of the altar.

Despite all our efforts, the "forces" grew stronger. I put Marcy behind me on a stool next to the front door. One of the invisible "things" approached me and stopped. That's when I made my mistake: I began to feel angry toward this being, power center or whatever it was, that seemed to be after this innocent child. As my emotion grew, the entity simply fed on the psychic energy I was releasing and grew stronger. It got around me and threw Marcy across the living room.

The unseen companion

Marcy ran back to me, crying. Finally, as the cloud inundated the whole interior of the house and as my physical strength waned, I ordered everyone outside. They needed no prodding. Luckily for us, the police had cleared away the crowds and cordoned off both ends of Lindley Street. Crowds at each end of the street saw us leave the house, though, and muttering broke out. It was about 8 p.m. and quite dark and cold, with a light sleet falling. Several neighbors stared helplessly from their front yards. I could hear a voice in the crowd preaching something about this all being a "sign of the end," although I'm sure it wasn't the "end" I was hoping for just then. I said the Lord's Prayer with the Goodins, then left them shivering on the front walk as I ran to a nearby house to find a telephone.

Apparently I wasn't alone. A dog came leaping out of someone's backyard, barking wildly. It got to within two feet of me, abruptly yelped and ducked behind some bushes, its tail between its legs. Several cats stared for a moment, then scurried away in terror.

I came to the house, and a wide-eyed little boy answered the door. "Mommy," he called, "the priest wants to use the phone!" Even here everyone seemed to think I was Fr. Charbonneau. The people were sympathetic, but as I stepped toward the phone, something rang the doorbell and knocked three times. "Mommy, there's nobody there!" the boy cried.

"You want to make a bet, kid?" I replied.

The Warrens left their home as soon as I called, but it took them nearly an hour and a half to get back through the suburbs to Lindley Street, thanks to the traffic and crowds. The Goodin house had become a five-star tourist attraction. When the Warrens finally arrived at about 9:15, we all re-entered the house. Things were quiet. When we turned on the radio, a newscaster was speculating about why we had left the house. Two reporters from WNAB Radio in Bridgeport arrived at about 9:30.

While I recounted the evening's events to those who hadn't been there, a mirror in Marcy's room fell and the kitchen table turned over twice. On three different occasions, three knocks sounded at the back door. No one was there. The drapes in the living room kept falling to the floor and the portable television there turned around every few minutes. At one point, Marcy was sitting in the kitchen and her chair began to rise. Since I was standing behind her, I grabbed the chair and pushed it back down.

We decided that an exorcism of the house would have to be performed by someone as soon as possible. Shortly after midnight, the Warrens and I, bleary-eyed and hungry, left the Goodin home, planning to return that afternoon (Tuesday, November 26) at about 1:30 p.m. Marcy kissed me and made me promise to come back.

"How can we ever thank you?" Laura Goodin said as she hugged the Warrens and me. As if to say farewell, the coffee table jumped across the living room as we walked out the front door.

After another few hours on the Warrens' living-room couch, I decided to go home to East Hartford to rest, shower and talk with my pastor. The Warrens had to go to Hartford on business. We agreed to meet back at the Goodin house at 2 p.m.

Marcy gets the rap

As my 1968 Ford sped east on Interstate 84, I tuned the radio to WCBS in New York —and I couldn't believe what I heard. The announcer was saying the Bridgeport police had declared the poltergeist a hoax perpetrated by Marcy! Every station I could get said the same thing.

The Warrens heard about this only after they got to Hartford. But when they arrived home at about 11:30 a.m., the chaos really began. Phone calls to Bridgeport police headquarters produced no answers, and even the Goodins' phone was answered by a policeman. The Goodins refused to speak with the Warrens. When they went back to Lindley Street, a policeman refused them entry, so they went to a friend's home in the city to listen to the radio and try more phone calls.

I arrived at Lindley Street at 2:30 p.m. and stood aghast on the front steps as Laura Goodin ordered a policeman to throw me off the property. I finally met the Warrens back at their home at about 5 p.m.

This is what had happened: The police had entered the Goodin house within minutes of our departure the previous night. Tougher minds at headquarters had decided that this ghostly ruckus had to end once and for all so that order could be restored in that part of the city. Veteran police interrogators grilled Marcy. Ultimately, according to police reports, she "confessed" to having perpetrated a hoax. Police Superintendent Joseph A. Walsh announced first thing Tuesday morning that the Bridgeport "poltergeist" was a child's prank.

The Warrens' phone didn't stop ringing all that evening. Calls came in from reporters as far away as Australia and western Canada. One caller, from the Toronto *Globe and Mail*, claimed that Fr. Charbonneau was now denying that he had witnessed phenomena in the house. This, of course, proved untrue. Another caller told us that Marcy had been taken to the Fairfield Hills Hospital near Bridgeport and was under psychiatric observation. These were only the first of many rumors that circulated in the media for months.

At 7 p.m., Ed Warren and I were guests on the three-hour Tiny Markel Show, a call-in program on WNAB radio. Virtually all callers agreed with us that the sudden police declaration of a "hoax" was hard to swallow, no matter what the explanation for the Lindley Street happenings might be.

The fur flies

Inane accusations were hurled against us from Lindley Street and police headquarters during the rest of November and early December. Believe it or not, these included: That the candy I'd bought on Monday afternoon was "drugged" and somehow caused the phenomena or caused Marcy to cause the phenomena; that Ed Warren had caused the events from his own home by witchcraft; and that all the witnesses had been put under some sort of "spell."

How any of these goofy charges were easier to believe than the truth is beyond me to this day. Of course, the silliest accusation of all was that a 10-year-old could fool large numbers of reliable, highly trained people for days by tossing around huge objects in a tiny house without being seen.

In any case, Fr. Charbonneau had become so well known that fan mail addressed simply to "Fr. Bill, Bridgeport, Conn." was forwarded to him without ado.

Faces at the Window

To the best of my knowledge, not one witness, including the policemen who were there, has ever retracted a story, and all those who were asked vouched for the professional way in which the Warrens, Fr. Charbonneau and I handled ourselves. The Warrens and a number of other witnesses publicly refuted the police version. Although fuming, I remained silent for years, again for the sake of anonymity.

Thus ended that segment of the haunting on Lindley Street. Over the remainder of 1974, the story, along with the battle between the Warrens and the police, died out in the press. Ed got a letter from the Goodins' lawyer warning him — and me — not to use the Goodins' name in any lectures. And on Lindley Street, Laura Goodin was shutting the door in the face of anyone who resembled a reporter.

Apparently, the poltergeist was far from banished. According to a number of reliable sources, the family's ordeal continued. Mrs. Goodin told a friend that her husband had to plant their Christmas tree in concrete because it kept moving. Reportedly, some of the furniture had to be wired down.

A new investigation

By January 1975, an investigative team from what was then the Duke University Parapsychology Laboratory had worked out a deal with the family and the police to go to the house and conduct a thorough investigation of its own. The deal was that no findings would be released until one year from the date of their investigation. Those involved were Jerry Solfvin and Keith Harary (later associated with the graduate parapsychology program at John F. Kennedy University in San Francisco), along with Boyce Batey, a lecturer and Connecticut resident affiliated with the Spiritual Frontiers Fellowship. One of these men later told me that the Goodins had vehemently denied any hoax and insisted that Marcy had nothing to do with the events.

Free of the media circus, these investigators approached the situation in a hard-nosed, scientific fashion. They administered a number of psychological tests to Mr. and Mrs. Goodin and conducted extensive interviews with witnesses, including me. Interestingly, all paranormal phenomena apparently ceased while the Duke people were in the house; they saw nothing unusual.

In the end, even these investigators threw up their hands over the inconsistency of witness reports, the Goodin family's highly charged emotions and no definite results from tests for psychokinesis (see glossary.) Years later Dr. Solfvin wrote me, "The case was never published by us for a variety of reasons. In fact, we never even wrote an 'in-house' report on it."

Late in January 1975, the Goodins were persuaded to appear on a local radio show, where they denied the hoax allegation and reports that Marcy was undergoing psychiatric treatment. They also said that paranormal events continued in the house.

In early February, a "For Sale" sign appeared in front of the house on Lindley Street. It took time, but the place finally sold, and the Goodins vanished from the public eye. As far as I could determine, nothing paranormal happened at the address after the Goodins left. How, when or if they got rid of their poltergeist are questions someone else will have to answer.

What's the answer?

Looking back at the Bridgeport poltergeist case, I think that the basic explanation we reached at the time was pretty close to the truth: Marcy was the origin and center of a classic poltergeist incident. She literally and unconsciously created a poltergeist or linked up with some extra-dimensional entity or entities to create one. Her personality was "textbook": A lonely, introverted, frustrated but intelligent child overshadowed by domineering parents and about to enter puberty.

While the *circumstances* accompanying the violent phenomenon of the poltergeist are fairly consistent from case to case, the *process* is little understood. Plenty of children are lonely and frustrated, but only a tiny fraction produce poltergeists.

Then there are the heavy objects tossed about during such episodes. In the laboratory, subjects trying to exert psychokincsis so far have succeeded in moving only very light objects, and for tiny distances. We certainly could revolutionize transportation if we discovered the poltergeist's secrets!

There also are nagging questions about our experience in the house on the night of November 25, when we felt entities "arriving" and moving about.

One possible clue in this mystery: Even under relatively controlled conditions, the literal creation of an entity seems to have occurred. In several well documented cases, groups of parapsychology students have, apparently through group concentration, created -- or perhaps unconsciously linked up with -- entities that have responded to questions and even, in a few cases, been photographed.

Today I'm very open to the possibility that certain extra-dimensional life forms -- easily equated with the "evil spirits" of world folklore -- may feed off of and gain strength from people, especially people in some sort of emotional distress and pumping out vast amounts of psychic energy. Under the right circumstances, these entities might well contribute to the heftier poltergeist phenomena if they get enough to "eat" from their victims. Remember: In the earliest vampire folklore, they weren't blood-sucking noblemen like Dracula, but life-sucking ghosts like poltergeists.

We're slowly learning, as the eminent British astronomer Sir Fred Hoyle believes, that life -- ever present and infinitely varied -- is the rule in the universe, not the exception. The existence of entities upon whom time and space (which Einstein proved are relative anyway) have little or no hold is not only possible but, my researches over the years have convinced me, a certainty.

Faces at the Window

In 1974 our conclusions were colored by our religious views, and we seriously thought that demonic entities in the Biblical sense were involved. In a way, maybe we weren't so far from the truth.

But even after all these years, I remember the very clear impression of *neutrality* when facing the "entities" that night in the Goodin house. They conveyed a feeling of neither good nor evil. They seemed almost sterile. While their treatment of Marcia seemed far from neutral, the girl was never physically hurt. As a matter of fact, Mrs. Goodin's broken toe and my minor leg wound were the only actual injuries that occurred through the entire brouhaha, as far as I know.

Paranormal investigation has taught me that there really is nothing more powerful than faith: Depending on what you believe, you can experience either the divine or the demonic. Around the world, cases of poltergeists and hauntings seem to take on religious characteristics only when the people involved are strong religious believers. That's when it's time to call in counselors of their own faiths, not because the faith is literally true but because *people's faith makes it true.*

All the more reason to believe that the subject is the psychic source from which the phenomena and any entities involved gain their ongoing power.

I'm not trying to denigrate or water down people's faiths. On the contrary, even theoretical physics hints at the fact that the power of faith is far more real in a far more practical way than many people think. It's a vivid tribute to the idea that God takes us "where we're at," and refuses to be limited by man-made perceptions and parameters.

Faces at the Window

2

The Vampires of Southern New England

An original version of this story appeared as "The Undead in Rhode Island" in the August 1985 issue of FATE magazine. Original elements are used here by permission of Llewellyn Worldwide, Ltd.

Faces at the Window

Mercy should have known better than to hire anyone from the Nooseneck Hill country, for that remote bit of backwoods was then, as now, a seat of the most uncomfortable superstitions. As late as 1892, an Exeter community exhumed a dead body and ceremoniously burnt its heart in order to prevent certain alleged visitations injurious to the public health and peace.

Thus wrote author Howard Phillips Lovecraft in *The Shunned House*, a tale of vampirism written in 1924 and set in his native Providence, Rhode Island. Most readers don't know that, while the story itself is fiction, the aside quoted above tells of a happening that is true in every ghoulish detail. And this was only one of a number of such incidents known to have taken place in New England between the Revolutionary War period and the 20th century. Indeed, a kind of vampire mania seems to have gripped parts of the region from time to time during these years: a sort of Salem witchcraft hysteria directed against the dead.

Each of our six New England states has had its vampire cases. Vermont media were reporting on a Burlington vampire cult as recently as 1992. But several of the most striking incidents occurred in eastern Connecticut and Rhode Island in the period between roughly 1770 and 1900.

Belief in vampires, in one form or another, has filtered down from the remote past. Vampires are mentioned in the lore of ancient Sumeria, Babylon, Greece, Rome and Israel and are found in mythologies as diverse as those of Brazil, China and the Rocky Mountains of North America. Of course, the world's vampire capital has always been central and eastern Europe. The vampires that supposedly haunted New England, as well as the steps people took against them, corresponded almost exactly with the general folk belief of central Europe. In the known Rhode Island and Connecticut cases the "vampires" were believed to be life-sucking ghosts that inhabited bodies of the dead and preyed only on

Faces at the Window

members of the dead persons' families.

How these beliefs crossed the Atlantic and became implanted in the minds of these 18th- and 19th-century New England farmers, hardheaded children of the Puritans, remains a mystery. No eastern Europeans are known to have settled in Rhode Island or eastern Connecticut before the mid-19th century, so immigrant influence could hardly have been a factor. Vampires didn't become popular in literature and drama until the early 1800s.

Michael E. Bell, Rhode Island's official folklorist, has documented at least nine vampire cases in that state alone. He suggests that these beliefs were always present, part of our "Indo-European heritage."

"Mundane stories don't get passed on (from one generation to another.) It's the amazing stories that do," Dr. Bell says.

Among New England's first known cases were several gruesome little affairs in eastern Connecticut in the last 30 years of the 18th century. At least one took place in the 1770s in the small town of Jewett City, Connecticut, not far from the borders of the aptly-named Nooseneck Hill region in nearby Rhode Island. In his book *These Plantations* (1937), J. Earl Clauson mentions this hair-raising event, which apparently took place shortly before the outbreak of the Revolution. He records only that "a corpse was disinterred and burned to destroy the vampire that inhabited it."

A grisly find

In 1991, some boys were playing at a gravel quarry near Griswold, Connecticut, not far from Jewett City, when a skull suddenly tumbled down a hillside and landed at their feet. They ran home in terror and, not long afterward, the matter was in the hands of archaeologists from the University of Connecticut. It seems that the quarry had nearly overtaken a Walton family burial ground. When the graves were excavated, skeletons were uncovered that indicated the mutilation of several bodies after burial, sometime around 1800. Experts agreed that they had been the posthumous victims of vampire hunters.

Apparently, at least some of these incidents were reported in now-vanished local newspapers, since Clauson wrote that "no sooner were the words off the press than reports began to come in of vampirism in Rhode Island."

"Little Rhody" is only 48 miles long and 37 miles wide (a 1983 *Wall Street Journal* article called it a "smudge" on the roadmap from New York City to Cape Cod) and much of the area around upper Narragansett Bay is heavily urbanized. But north of that region the land rises into rolling hills that frame the lovely Blackstone River as it courses drowsily down to the tidewater from Massachusetts. It is a land of rocky woods, broad hilltops and mill villages where author Lovecraft loved to wander in the 1920s and 1930s. Today, the villages prosper as "bedroom communities" for commuters to Boston, some 40 miles to the northeast.

Town Council says 'yes'

It was here, in Cumberland on the Massachusetts border, that a striking but little-known vampire case occurred in 1796. And the record of it sits to this day in the vault at the Cumberland Town Hall.

On February 8th of that year, one Stephen Staples petitioned the Town Council for permission to dig up the body of Abigail Staples, his 23-year-old daughter, because, he said, she was rising from the grave each night to drain the lives of her eight brothers and sisters.

This is from Volume 4, page 1 of the Town Council records:

> **Mr. Stephen Staples of Cumberland appeared before this body and prayed that he might have liberty granted unto him to dig up the body of his daughter, Abigail Staples, late of Cumberland, a single woman, deceased, in order to try an experiment on Lavina Chace, wife**

Faces at the Window

38

of Stephen Chace, which said Lavina was sister to the said Abigail, deceased. Which being duly considered, voted and resolved that the said Stephen Staples have liberty to dig up the body of the said Abigail, deceased, and after trying the experiment as aforesaid that he bury the body of the said Abigail in a decent manner.

-Photo by Paul F. Eno

One of dozens of old family burying grounds in Cumberland, Rhode Island. No-one is sure where Abigail Staples actually is buried.

Lavina and other Staples children evidently were wasting away, almost certainly with the highly infectious disease we know today as pulmonary tuberculosis. In those days it was called "consumption," was feared though little understood, and crops up time and again in these incidents.

The "experiment" Staples performed was typical of the "remedy" in New England's vampire cases. It was believed that the cycle of consumption and death could be stopped if the body of the suspected vampire was exhumed, the bones broken to prevent its moving about, and the heart burned. To help ailing family members, the smoke from the fire might be inhaled or the ashes from the heart actually ingested in some way.

Faces at the Window

In the Nooseneck Hill country

Some 35 miles south of Cumberland, past the developed region of Providence, Cranston and Warwick, is a wide land of hills, scrubby fields and second-growth woodland. At its heart is the Nooseneck Hill country referred to by Lovecraft, where I once lived and which includes the towns of Exeter, West Greenwich and part of Coventry. Despite a few housing developments near Interstate 95 and other main roads, the area still is surprisingly isolated and looks much as it did in the 19th century. It is beautiful country for those whose taste runs to the austere, with wide hilltops covered with gnarled trees and deep glens where sunlight penetrates only on winter days. It is not an unfitting setting for vampires.

The deadly dream

In an 1888 Providence publication known as *Book Notes* (Vol. 5, No. 7), we find a detailed account from the publication's editor, Sidney S. Rider. He doesn't identify the location, but there's some reason to believe that the incident he describes took place in West Greenwich in the mid-1770s.

Although he strongly implies that the name is a pseudonym, Rider identifies the family involved as the Stukeleys, headed by a handsome, well-to-do young farmer whom the locals nicknamed "Snuffy Stuke" because of the butternut-brown jacket he liked to wear. Mr. and Mrs. Stukeley were blessed with 14 children, several of whom had already reached their upper teens. One night, Snuffy had a simple dream that greatly, if inexplicably, disturbed him. He dreamed that he was the owner of a large orchard, half of whose trees suddenly died.

Soon the dream's meaning became all too apparent. Within a short time, his oldest daughter, Sarah, developed what seemed to be consumption and rapidly wasted away. She died and was laid to rest in the family burying ground on the Stukeley property.

Faces at the Window

Snuffy's subconscious fears were not buried with Sarah, and his strange dream kept recurring. Before long, the next-oldest daughter contracted the same disease and began to wither away as her sister had. But this time, there was a big difference: The terrified girl complained of nightly visits from her dead sister, whom she said "sat upon some portion of the body, causing great pain and misery." Then she herself died.

And so it went. One after another, the children sickened and died until six were gone and another, the first son, was taken ill. At the same time Mrs. Stukeley started complaining of nightly visits from Sarah. The grief-stricken, terrified family held a council with "the most learned people," presumably local officials, physicians and clergy. After some discussion, it was decided that a vampire was at work. Neighbors were called in to help, and with picks and spades opened the graves of the six dead children.

When the bodies were viewed, five proved to be in an advanced state of decomposition. But one, the body of Sarah, the first to die, reportedly was in a remarkable state indeed. Sarah's eyes were open and fixed, her hair and nails had grown, and her heart and arteries were filled with fresh blood. It was clear to all that the cause of their trouble lay before them.

Wasting no time, they cut the heart from Sarah's body and from the bodies of the five others and burned the organs on a rock in front of the Stukeley home. The bodies then were reburied. It was a remedy right out of the dark mountains of Transylvania.

At last, peace descended on the troubled house, but not before a seventh victim had died. This was the sick son, a promising young farmer who had recently married and lived on an adjoining farm. He already had been too far gone. Thus was the dream of Snuffy Stukeley fulfilled, with the "orchard" of his children depleted by half.

Rider ends his narrative with a chilling statement: "Those

Faces at the Window

from whom these facts were obtained little suspected the foreign character of the origin of the extraordinary circumstances which they described, but extraordinary as they are, there are nevertheless those still living who religiously believe in them."

'I am waiting and watching for you.'

Indeed, a nearly identical case took place in West Greenwich nearly a century later, in 1889. Here, the body of the unfortunately Nelly L. Vaughn, who had died that year at the age of 19, was exhumed and her heart burned a few months after her death.

While few details of the case are known, the spooky epitaph on Nelly's gravestone, "I am waiting and watching for you," has sent chills up people's spines for over 100 years. Somehow, the grave became such a magnet for curiousity seekers and cultists, including some students from the nearby University of Rhode Island, that town officials had to ask state troopers for help.

As recently as 1979, a West Greenwich town official complained to me that pranksters still managed to find the rural cemetery to vandalize and otherwise desecrate the grave of the hapless Nelly, especially at Halloween.

"It's horrible," the official said. "They ought to leave that poor girl alone."

As to Nelly's epitaph, almost certainly placed on the stone before the "vampire" incident, I'm sure the family had no intention of conjuring up thoughts of the undead. Just the opposite: Epitaphs such as Nelly's were quite common as sober, pious and deliberate reminders that death looks neither at age nor rank.

'A family of respectable surroundings'

In his 1888 account of the Sarah Stukeley affair, author Rider wrote ominously that, since he wrote his story, "another similar case in Wakefield, R.I., has come to my knowl-

-Photo by Paul F. Eno
Lewis Peck of Exeter, Rhode Island, at the gravestone of his relative, alleged 19ᵗʰ-century vampire Mercy Brown.

edge; and still another now is in contemplation in a family of respectable surroundings, several of the members of which have recently died."

The "family of respectable surroundings" were the Browns of Exeter, on whose subsequent actions Lovecraft based his

Faces at the Window

aside in *The Shunned House* and probably got the idea for the story itself.

In my opinion, this is the quintessential case of New England vampirism. It's striking not only for its bizarre nature but for the fact that it took place on the threshold of the 20th century, was well documented, and because descendents of those involved can talk about it even today. As if that weren't enough, there is some evidence that the case helped inspire Abraham "Bram" Stoker, author of *Dracula*, to write that most classic of all vampire sagas, in 1897.

The Browns of Exeter were not country bumpkins. They were well-off, respected farming people related to some of the most distinguished figures of Rhode Island's colonial history, including the founder of Brown University. As far as can be learned, Clauson's was the first published account of the Brown case in this century, and it was retold in *Yankee* magazine in 1970, to be republished in that monthly's book *Mysterious New England* in 1971. I wrote about it in *Fate* magazine in 1986, and the Rhode Island media often drag it out as a sensational feature at Halloween. While there are some variations in the accounts, the following has been handed down in the family of Lewis Peck of Exeter, whose grandmother, a Brown, recalled the incredible incident:

Mrs. Mary E. Brown died, apparently of consumption, on December 8, 1883, leaving her husband, George, with one son and several daughters. A mere six months later, on June 6, 1884, the oldest daughter, 20-year-old Mary, died of the same disease. Then, around 1888, the son Edwin, a store clerk in another part of Exeter, suddenly fell ill. Once again it was consumption. In an effort to recover, Edwin took a trip to Colorado, where he fared no better. Declining rapidly, Edwin returned to Rhode Island, only to find that his 19 year-old sister Mercy (note the character of that name in the Lovecraft story) also had contracted the disease and was in even worse shape than he was.

Mercy succumbed in January 1892 as Edwin was still bat-

Faces at the Window

tling for his life. At their wits' end, 12 of the Browns got together to decide what could be done for Edwin. They considered it extremely odd that Edwin, a husky, strapping young man previously noted for his strength and health, should be wasting away. In due course, the Browns decided unanimously that a vampire must be draining the life out of him — a vampire that probably resided in the grave of one of the three deceased family members. They undoubtedly were aware of the local traditions about such things.

So on a cold March day in 1892, a grim assembly arrived at the Chestnut Hill Cemetery in Exeter, behind the Baptist church of that name. The remains of Mrs. Brown and Mary, buried for years, proved to be only skeletons. But in Mercy's grave was a startling find. Not only did the body look in the pink of health, with blood in the heart and arteries, but it had turned over part way in the coffin.

Undaunted by the fact that Mercy had been the third to die, not the first, the vampire-hunters cut the girl's heart from her body and burned it on a rock that still can be seen not far from the grave. Then all three bodies were reburied, and the ashes of the heart gathered up, for Edwin's doctor, a full believer in the vampire theory, had prescribed for him the ashes of his sister's heart, dissolved in medicine. This grotesque remedy evidently did Edwin no good; he died shortly thereafter.

Inspiration for Stoker's Dracula

This was the last known case of "vampirism" in Rhode Island, and it is by no means forgotten locally. Mercy's grave can be seen behind the still-active Chestnut Hill Baptist Church, as can those of Mrs. Brown and Mary. Mercy's stone, stolen in 1996 but since recovered, stands out because the pious epitaph has been carefully and cleanly effaced. Peck, who talks about Mercy only if prodded, says he doesn't know who brings the small flowers that occasionally can be seen there.

Faces at the Window

But the belief that Mercy really was a vampire persisted, and still silently persists among certain old-timers of that region. Peck hedges as to his own position on the matter, saying only that "there are still a lot of people around here who believe in some pretty strange things." He recalls clearly, though, that "my mother and grandmother told us never, ever to touch [Mercy's] gravestone."

He says he will never forget one incident in particular. It took place in the early 1960s when Peck was in his 30s. "I was in back of the church hall with a friend of mine," he says. "It was about 11 p.m., and suddenly we saw this great big ball of light right over Mercy's grave. I was scared to death! I've never seen anything like it before or since."

In a compelling twist to the Brown affair, a newspaper clipping about the case reportedly was found among Bram Stoker's *Dracula* notes after the author died in 1912.

What's the answer?

There are, of course, only two general explanations for New England's vampire hysteria. One is that vampires as understood in folk belief exist and can be dealt with as described. The other, much more credible explanation is that these beliefs were bred and reinforced by certain little-understood natural phenomena, particularly tuberculosis and its highly contagious nature.

This much is clear at least: in virtually every folk belief there is some grain of truth, however distorted it may have become through centuries of retelling. A number of scholars, including Daniel Farson (a grandnephew of *Dracula* author Stoker), have speculated that premature burial is responsible for much of the belief in vampires the world over. He notes that even today it is not all that easy to tell when someone is really dead.

Looking at the Brown case, about which we know the most, we could set up the following gruesome but plausible scenario: Mercy was not really dead when she was laid in her coffin. Because it was January, the ground almost certainly was frozen and, as was the custom in New England until recently, the coffin was placed in a receiving vault at the cemetery until the early spring thaw. In a short time, Mercy either froze to death or suffocated but not before she turned partly over. Frozen, the body and the remaining blood would be spared decomposition. When the thaw came, the coffin was buried, only to be disturbed by the vampire hunters a short time later. Of course, they found the body perfectly preserved.

Still, this would not explain Mercy's looking "in the pink of health," if indeed this is not just an embellishment to the story from a later date. Also, one would think that the above explanation would have occurred to those who did the digging that day.

In any event, such an explanation would certainly not apply to each of the thousands of such cases that have been recorded around the world. There are, however, other precedents for the incorruption of bodies after long periods. Farson points out that burial in volcanic soil usually will result in a perfect state of preservation (although the soil of the Nooseneck Hill country has been more influenced by glaciers than volcanoes).

Both the Eastern Orthodox and Roman Catholic Churches use bodily incorruption as a major, but not absolutely necessary, criterion for an individual's canonization, and the bodies of these people almost always are exhumed for this purpose. There are well attested cases in both ancient and modern times in which such bodies have been found, after years and sometimes centuries of burial, in graves filled with fresh flowers or fragrant myrrh. This phenomenon, which defies explanation, is not confined to Christianity. Instances of it are attributed to the holy people of a number of faiths.

In any event, the differences between the Stukeley and Brown cases certainly point out the difficulties of arriving at a single explanation for vampire phenomena. In one case, (if the story can be considered accurate after more than 200 years) there was a steady progression of deaths, with the first victim turning out to be the "vampire" who made apparitional visitations to family members. In the other, it was the last of the dead who became the vampire, and there are no reports of her actual appearance to any victims.

We can conclude only that the New England vampire cases were the sad results of fatal diseases coupled with bizarre backwoods superstitions. Researchers have stumbled on most of these cases by chance, and it's chilling to think how widespread the beliefs and "remedies" must have been for quite a long period in New England's history.

Faces at the Window

3

Connecticut's Village of Voices

An original version of this story appeared as "Bara Hack: Village of Voices" in the October and November 1985 issues of FATE magazine. Original elements are used here by permission of Llewellyn Worldwide, Ltd.

Faces at the Window

Buried deep in Windham County, known as Connecticut's "Quiet Corner," is the scene of one of New England's least known but most unusual hauntings, and probably one of the world's most noteworthy. Set amid dense woods in the Town of Pomfret, the "Lost Village," "Lost Village of the Hills" or "Village of Voices" has long been known locally as a place of virtually incessant paranormal activity. Standing almost anywhere within its square half-mile, one often hears shouts, mutterings, the rattle of wagons and other sounds as if it were a normal day in the lives of the long-dead people of this abandoned settlement.

In 1971 and 1972, the Lost Village was investigated by a group of parapsychology students. I led this investigation, the first by the group that would later become the Psychical Research Team of New England, now defunct.

We could discover only a little about the Lost Village's mysterious history. As best we could tell, the first settler, Obadiah Higginbotham (1750-1803), a deserter from the British army, fled Cranston, Rhode Island, for the hills of Pomfret to avoid separation from his American bride, Dorcas. Such desertions were quite common in colonial America, even after the American Revolution began. The British regular of the day almost always was drawn from the poorest of Britain's poor, and there was little to go back to on the other side of the Atlantic.

Higginbotham and his Yankee bride must have fled from Rhode Island at about the time the Revolution got under way, since their fourth child, Darius, was born in Pomfret that year. At about the same time, Jonathan Randall also moved from Cranston to Pomfret. Presumably, there was some connection between these two families, whose scions are buried in a little cemetery in the woods above the Lost Village.

They cleared the land and built their first houses in this wild and lonely spot above a natural basin formed by

Faces at the Window

Mashomoquet Brook. Later, a stone dam was built below the bluff on which Obadiah's house stood, forming a pond that later provided water power for the Higginbotham Linen Wheels mill. This little factory made spinning wheels and looms as late as the Civil War.

The Higginbothams and Randalls apparently were Welsh, and they called their settlement Bara-Hack, "breaking of bread" in the Cymric (Welsh) tongue.

The well-to-do Randalls had slaves to work in the culti- vated fields and storage barns around the main houses in Bara-Hack. According to local sources, the haunting was first rumored among the slaves. After the first interments (of a baby and some slaves) took place in the little burial

-Photo by Robert Zachary

A large hickory tree now grows out of the cellar hole where, it is believed, British army deserter Obadiah Higginbotham built his house in Pomfret, Connecticut, as the American Revolution began.

Faces at the Window

ground in the early 1800s, the workers claimed that at dusk, ghosts could be seen there reclining in the branches of a certain elm tree. Remember this, for it comes back to haunt us later.

As with so many other New England settlements, the residents either moved away or were laid to rest one by one in their little cemetery. By the end of the Civil War, Higginbotham Linen Wheels had given way to its large competitors in the textile cities of Connecticut, Massachusetts and Rhode Island. A few fields still were under cultivation, but the sheep and cows were fast disappearing as their owners found better farms and pastures elsewhere. The last interments in the cemetery took place in the 1890s.

Into the 20th century

Although there were no living residents, peculiar things were happening at Bara-Hack early in the 20th century as the woods finished reclaiming the settlement. The only published record of this period that I could find was in a little-known but delightful book by naturalist Odell Shepard, a professor at Hartford's Trinity College, whose *The Harvest of a Quiet Eye* (1927) describes the author's visit to what already was known as the Village of Voices. Shepard wrote:

> **Here had been their houses, represented today by a few gaping cellar holes out of which tall trees were growing; but here *is* the Village of Voices. For the place is peopled still . . . . Although there is no human habitation for a long distance round about and no one goes there except the few who go to listen, yet there is always a hum and stir of human life . . . .**
>
> **They hear the laughter of children at play . . . the voices of mothers who have long been dust calling their children into the homes that are now mere holes in the ground. They hear vague snatches of song . . . and the rumble of heavy**

Faces at the Window

-Photo by Harry A. Chase

Mashomoquet Brook where it passes the ruins of the former Higginbotham Linen Wheels mill at Bara-Hack. This is the area in which investigators heard the laughter of unseen children moving rapidly up and down the brook.

> **wagons along an obliterated road. It is as though sounds were able in this place to get round that incomprehensible corner, to pierce that mysterious soundproof wall that we call Time.**

I didn't discover Shepard's book until long after the Lost Village investigation. If I had, my team and I might have been better prepared for what we experienced there.

During the quarter century or so between Shepard's visit (in the early 1920s) and the late 1940's, we have only rumors and snatches of stories about the haunting of Bara-Hack. Among the tales of voices are scattered sightings of ghostly bluish shapes flitting among the trees at dusk, especially near the burying ground.

In the summer of 1948, Harry A. Chase, 45 years old and a lifelong resident of Pomfret, went to stroll through the Lost Village as he had done countless times before on quiet afternoons. This time, though, he brought his new box camera to get some snapshots of the cellar holes and old grave-stones.

When the prints were developed, Chase thought that something was wrong with the film or that somebody was playing tricks on him. The clerk at the drugstore sent the prints back to the photo lab to be checked, only to learn that there was no mistake. The whitish blobs and ghostly streaks among the trees really were on the film, right there in black and white.

A skeptic with no knowledge of psychic photography (see glossary), Chase became profoundly curious about what could have caused such a phenomenon. These were by no means the last such photos he took there. One especially remarkable shot, taken in the late 1960s, shows Chase and a friend sitting on the stone steps leading from the Higginbotham home site to the stone dam. Two ghostly blobs or orbs appear in front of their legs, and one can see right through the legs to the stone behind! Sadly, that and many other photos disappeared after Chase's death in 1974.

Harry A. Chase of Pomfret, who was to be our guide at the Village of Voices in 1971, took this photo of the Higginbotham-Randall burying ground in 1948. Note the odd streaks in the left foreground.

Faces at the Window

While glancing through a weekday edition of the *Hartford Courant* in November 1970, I first saw mention of Pomfret's Lost Village. Besides reprinting one of the psychic photos, the article mentioned Harry Chase as a local historian who knew as much about the site as anyone alive.

I had recently become a serious student of the paranormal. With a group of fellow students and several local experts in the field, I was in the process of forming an investigative group that would be highly mobile and capable of investigating and documenting many types of paran-

Harry Chase of Pomfret and his formidable poodle in 1971.

ormal phenomena. The Lost Village struck me as an appropriate place for our first investigation. Funds and equipment had just been obtained through our parent organization, the United Acadian Federation, a cultural, scientific and public-service group made up primarily of students.

Our expedition arrives

We arranged to meet with Chase, and on August 30, 1971, six of us, including a photography expert and a sound technician, made the beautiful trip from Hartford to Pomfret. After setting up camp in a nearby state park, we sought out the scholarly recluse, then 68, in his rustic cottage at the edge of an orchard. After a fascinating conversation about local history, the Lost Village and its alleged ghosts, we set out for the site, some six miles away.

"I'm not saying there are any such things as ghosts, but I'm not saying there aren't, either," Chase said on the way. "I'll admit I've heard some awfully strange things there myself."

He noted that many people had been to the Village of

Faces at the Window

Voices and heard nothing unusual. One daring young man had even spent the night in the cemetery itself and had "slept like a rock."

Our plan for the first of three expeditions was to explore and map the site. Having found what little we could about the place's history and people, we also planned to take numerous photos with both 35mm and 126 films, color and black and white. We further planned to spread out and observe the area at night, attempting to record any unusual sounds for later analysis.

Parking our vehicle just beyond Mashomoquet Brook, we followed an overgrown cart path into the dense woods, coming to the Lost Village itself after a quarter-mile walk. Before we came within sight of the ancient stone walls and overgrown cellar holes, though, several things besides the heat and insects affected all seven of us.

Sounds from the past

First of all, although the sun was bright, there seemed to be an overpowering sense of depression in the area. Second, even though the nearest residence was over a mile away (we had carefully checked this), we heard the constant barking of dogs, lowing of cows and an occasional human voice from the dense woods close at hand. Third, everyone noted a complete absence of birds, an unlikely circumstance for the place and time of year.

Even we skeptics couldn't help raising an eyebrow at such odd conditions. Nonetheless, we were fully prepared to find some sort of "rational" explanation for the happenings at the Lost Village.

Having arrived at about 2:45 p.m., we finished our initial exploration, mapping and photography at about five o'clock. We left, returning at about 7:15 p.m. to take up observation positions around the village. It was a beautiful late summer evening when we arrived at the old cellar hole that marked the former location of the main Higginbotham home. The

Faces at the Window

sense of depression still hung about the place, and hundreds of katydids had taken up their eerie, insistent buzzing. But as we set up recording equipment and assigned observation posts for the evening, another sound became increasingly evident. Alvin Leblanc, assistant team leader, noticed it first; then all of us in turn looked down the bluff toward the stone dam across Mashomoquet Brook.

It was laughter we heard — the laughter of a crowd of children: clear, bright and unmistakable. Hastily we turned on our recording equipment and sent two observers down the path to check the brook area. Oddly, the sounds seemed to move rapidly up and down the brook below our position. Odder still, the observers could see nothing but the dense woods. The sounds would not record.

Just to make sure of what we had heard, we sent Leblanc and our sound technician, Michael Devin, to search the area. The only possible source of any children's sounds was a 4H camp about a mile from our position in the woods. A check there revealed no children, however, only three counselors. The camp was in the opposite direction from where we had heard the sounds.

The rest of the evening proved uneventful, and we left at about 9:30 p.m. I say "uneventful" because we had long since grown accustomed to the "background noise" of cows, dogs and people. Back at our camp, we discussed plans for the following day, August 31. We didn't sleep at the Lost Village itself because we could not contact the property owners in New Haven to get their permission and, moreover, we made it a point never to sleep at the site of an investigation until we were sure what we were dealing with. Anyone who has had expensive equipment ruined by a poltergeist knows what I mean.

Blobs, streaks and faces

We spent the next day at the Lost Village, taking pictures and refining our map and notes, as well as at Harry Chase's

-Photo by Alvin Leblanc

When this photo was taken at the Bara-Hack burying ground, nobody saw the baby-like figure reclining in the branches, upper left, though a similar figure was seen there that night. The figure recalls 18th-century reports of ghosts reclining in the branches of trees at the same spot.

house comparing notes with him. But the best was yet to come; this was the evening we planned to spend at the cemetery itself.

We climbed the little hill above the cellar holes at about 7:30 p.m. and took up positions around the cemetery at dusk. We didn't have long to wait before things started to happen. Although six of us were stationed at different places around the cemetery's perimeter, we all later reported seeing the same things, and we saw them at the same times.

Throughout the three hours that we watched, we frequently saw bluish streaks or blobs moving through the trees. For over seven minutes we watched a bearded face suspended in the air over the cemetery's western wall, while in an elm tree over the northern wall we clearly saw a baby-like figure reclining on a branch. (Remember the nearly 200-year-old reports of ghosts reclining in elm trees?) Our cameras, set for time-lapse photography in the thin light of the waxing moon, clicked incessantly.

Exhausted and out of film, we reluctantly withdrew at about 10:30. As we passed the cellar holes, I happened to glance back toward the cemetery. Suspended in the path about 100 feet behind us was a ghostly blob. Was it saying "good-bye" or "good riddance?"

Ghostly 'extras'

The following week, our team met to discuss our findings and to see what conclusions we

-Photos by Paul F. Eno

According to photo analysis, the ghostly figures circled (inset) are not reflections. They include two figures and what appears to be a face. Interestingly, it was from that area that we heard voices during the Mercier "paralysis" episode on our second expedition that fall.

Faces at the Window

could draw. The photographs, checked and rechecked by an independent photo lab in East Hartford, Connecticut, showed some remarkable things.

Curiously, though, none of our night shots came out. But there was the baby-in-the-tree in a daytime shot, taken the afternoon before we actually saw it. Other "extras" included ghostly streaks, an image on a gravestone and the not uncommon "psychic light rod" phenomenon, rising from a gravestone and tipped with a blazing light. Unfortunately, none of our tapes held anything of interest, only the ever-present evening buzzing of the katydids.

Psychic residuum

Although it was difficult to be sure, our general conclusions were that the voices and other paranormal sounds were the result of some sort of psychic residuum, heard by all of us at once by telepathic means. How else could we explain the fact that the sounds wouldn't record? Rationally, we wanted to explain the other, visual phenomena by some similar process. But one strange, unscientific feeling kept us thinking that perhaps there really were such things as earthbound spirits and that maybe we were dealing with a whole village of them. It was especially difficult to explain this feeling in a group of skeptical students who were steeped in academics and theories of psi (see glossary) and who were trying to maintain, despite inexperience, as much cold objectivity as possible. The intense feeling of sadness we had felt at the Lost Village, the genuine emotional conviction that we were literally in contact with people from the past, haunted all of us.

Halloween visit

Our schedule brought us back to Pomfret on, ironically, October 30 and 31, 1971. We had deliberately replaced some of our team members to see if the newcomers would pick up the same impressions as the others. To help assure ob-

Faces at the Window

Above, a phenomenon than known as a "psychic light rod" rises from one of the gravestones at Bara-Hack. Below, a ghostly dagger seems fixed in the ground near the grave of Darius Higginbotham.

-Photo by Roland Mercier

Faces at the Window

jectivity, these new members, Marcel Mercier, Robert Zachary and Louis Letendre, were kept in the dark about everything but the vital statistics of the case.

Autumn had come to the Village of Voices. The feeling of sadness was more pronounced than before, although the "background noise" seemed much less than we had noted on our first trip. Harry Chase was on hand on that first overcast day to tell us about the experiences of other visitors who had seen and heard things there in August and September.

After reexamining the area that afternoon (we always tried to be on the lookout for evidence of fraud), we returned at dusk to see what we could hear or see. We got much more than we expected.

Terror in the night

Leaving Zachary and Letendre at the cellar holes with the recording equipment, the rest of us started toward the cemetery in the growing darkness. It was quite dark, with a pale, waxing moon, by the time we reached what should have been the cemetery. But try as we might, with spotlights flashing and steps retraced, we couldn't find it. We had been there at night before, the landmarks were familiar and we knew the terrain well by this time. It was as if the place had vanished.

Finally, flabbergasted and embarrassed, we radioed to the two men at the cellar holes to meet us halfway down the road and, together, we would try again to find the burial ground. But they had troubles of their own. It seemed that someone had pulled Bob Zachary's hat off his head while he was working near the Higginbotham cellar hole. The hat was neatly lodged on a branch high overhead. They were trying to get it down by means of flashlights and stones when we radioed. Bob didn't get his hat back until the next day. The two dropped what they were doing and joined us.

All six of us then moved into the black stillness toward

Faces at the Window

the burial ground. As we came to a spot that the next day proved to be not more than 100 feet from the gate, I turned around and saw that Letendre and Mercier had stopped. The rest of us turned back to see what was wrong, only to find Marcel huffing and puffing as if he were about to have a heart attack. He complained of a dry throat and a sensation of terrible coldness. His skin was clammy to the touch.

I was worried about his health and wanted to leave, but he protested that he was all right and wanted to go on. Then we found that it was physically impossible to pull him forward or to the left (the direction of the cemetery) while it was quite easy for him to move backwards and to the right. Suddenly, he broke out in a cold sweat and began to sob so hard that he doubled over onto his walking stick.

Mercier was a family man in his late 30s, a no-nonsense individual who worked for a major corporation and who was with us as an adviser on cameras and other equipment. He was by far the most skeptical member of the group. As he said in a radio interview on WINY, a Putnam, Connecticut, station, the next day, this experience profoundly changed his attitude toward the paranormal.

At our wits' end, a few of us started to pray out loud, which seemed to ease Mercier's condition. He didn't know why, he said, but something was telling him that we must not go to the cemetery that night. He didn't understand it. He wanted to go on but sensed that we mustn't.

Then we heard the voices...

At that point we heard the voices. It was a large group that couldn't have been more than 10 feet away in the direction of the cemetery. We could see nothing. All we could hear was the rising and falling of muttered conversation. We couldn't make out what was being said, but we agreed that it did sound like English.

After another vain attempt to pull Mercier along (four of us at once were unable to do so) and another bout of sob-

At least four images seem etched onto this print, taken at the Bara-Hack burying ground. It was taken with a Kodak Instamatic® 126 camera, however, which cannot double expose. When the photo first appeared in FATE magazine, people from all over the world wrote to the author stating that they could see dozens of faces. Internationally known psychical investigator Ed Warren once pronounced this one of the most remarkable psychic photographs of the 20th century.

bing, we decided to withdraw. Someone or something had gone to a great deal of trouble to keep us away from the Lost Village's burial ground that night, for what reason we will never know. Mercier said later that he'd "felt as if possessed."

Because the next day happened to be Halloween, our team became open game for publicity. We duly appeared on WINY to be interviewed by reporter David Silverman. The audience got an earful, what with the story of the previous night's events.

Faces at the Window

Peace seems to return

We could have left Pomfret that day with the satisfaction that we had documented a genuine and unique haunting. We could have used our information for endless speculation or for scholarly papers later in our academic careers. But we decided to make one more trip back to the Village of Voices because of that uncanny feeling of personal solidarity with the long-dead inhabitants, a feeling that had taken a strong hold on all of us.

We all went to a local church on that gray, chilly Sunday morning of October's last day, and that afternoon we again gathered at the Lost Village's little cemetery. This time we came without cameras, recording gear or scientific preconceptions. We came instead with loving concern for the people we believed were there and toward whom, I will presume to say, we had a feeling not unlike friendship. Many in the group were not particularly religious, but we brought a book of prayers and read some of them together as we sat on the ancient stonework of the gate.

As soon as we finished praying, several simple things happened. Perhaps there was no connection, but the praying lifted our spirits and, we felt, those of our invisible companions. Out came the sun, and all sorts of birds suddenly started to sing where we'd never heard so much as a chirp before. All at once, it seemed, the spirit of sadness and depression was gone. As we left the cemetery and walked down the path toward the cellar holes, however, we heard the sound. It was the rumbling of a wagon and the shouts of a team driver proceeding from the cemetery area and through the woods directly in front of us in a dense and completely impassable section. This lasted for nearly 10 minutes. Everyone heard it but saw nothing odd.

From all the information we gathered in the ensuing five years, there were no more ghostly streaks or blobs seen at the Lost Village and, as far as we learned, no more "extras" appeared in photos taken there.

Faces at the Window

Indeed, several of us returned to the Lost Village in June 1972, while on our way to investigate a case in Rhode Island. We just wanted to make sure that things were still peaceful. With the landowner's permission, we spent more than 30 hours at the Village of Voices, camped at the cemetery gate and found everything quiet. There weren't even any voices, although they still can be heard there, I'm told. I think it would be a pity if they were gone forever.

What's the answer?

Over the years, I've pondered my experiences at the Lost Village. The experience of personal solidarity and, indeed, love we felt for the people of the past has been unique in my 25 years of paranormal investigation. Truly, that feeling of closeness to those people is still with me. I've felt it again from time to time in similar cases, but never as poignantly as I did at Bara-Hack.

Nevertheless, I now feel that our belief about the possibilities of "earthbound spirits" missed the mark. As a matter of fact, I don't even believe in death anymore, so I certainly don't believe that ghosts are spirits of the dead.

Rather, I believe we can find an answer in quantum mechanics, which I discuss in the introduction to this book. I think that Bara-Hack may have been, and probably still is, what some Native Americans call a "thin place." It's a place where the boundaries between the physical and spiritual worlds (or, as theoretical physics might say, the boundaries between alternate universes, in some of which the people of Bara-Hack still carry on their daily lives) are "thin" or even nonexistent at times.

Indeed, author Odell Shepard may have been closer to the truth than he realized when he wrote of the voices piercing "that mysterious soundproof wall that we call Time."

So, as I sit at my desk and think of the Lost Village, as I often do, the lines from New England's own Henry Wadsworth Longfellow run through my mind:

Faces at the Window

The stranger at my fireside cannot see
the forms I see, nor the sounds I hear,
He but perceives what is,
While unto me, all that has been
is visible and clear.

****

Special Note: If you plan to visit Pomfret's Lost Village, forget it unless you have the landowner's permission. On my last visit, in 1994, I found the place wallpapered with "No Trespassing" signs, so I didn't get past the entrance to the old cart path. I fear and regret that this may be because of publicity generated by a nationally published article of mine in the 1980s, parts of which were reprinted in several books in America and Britain. Unfortunately, a number of curiosity-seeking readers apparently made their way to Pomfret and made pests of themselves to the point that the site now is closed to the public.

Faces at the Window

4

Trouble from the Ouija Board

Faces at the Window

Lucy Cormier was a pretty 15 year-old with long blond hair. After becoming interested in the ouija board a friend had given her as a present, she became fascinated by the "spirit world" and with the "spirit guide" she communicated with over the board, and by other divining methods. Her older brother became interested, too. After he joined the Navy, the family was startled by certain phenomena that began late in 1975 and early in 1976.

Phenomena seemed to follow Lucy around. On several occasions, members of the family saw a ghostly figure with long blonde hair, usually leaning over Lucy's bed while the girl was asleep. This even occurred at the family's vacation home on Block Island, Rhode Island. Loud bangings would be heard around the house, and minor poltergeist phenomena began to take place at the Cormier home in Glastonbury, Connecticut. While Lucy was visiting it, bizarre happenings also took place at an 18th-century home in nearby Coventry, Connecticut, in which her boyfriend's sister lived. An orange-glowing, ball-type apparition was seen on one of these occasions.

A concerned friend of Lucy's approached me after one of my lectures and asked for help.

Interestingly, Lucy thought the phenomena were fascinating, and she wasn't afraid in the least. As she told me herself, they brought her recognition, along with mystery and adventure in an otherwise ordinary life. After interviews and visits to both the Cormier residence and the Coventry house, it was clear that paranormal phenomena were taking place: I myself felt the "psychic cold," associated with these phenomena, witnessed sounds and minor poltergeist activity.

The first time I was being shown around the Coventry house, a venerable 17th century farmstead surrounded by fields and stables, I was accompanied by Lucy. "Something" followed us around the house, turning on lights as we went! At one point, I turned around and followed "it," led by the

Faces at the Window

trail of "psychic cold" it left. The "entity" led me into a corner room, then dissipated.

Would that all cases were so simple to cure: Prayers read with the Cormier family at their home and a blessing with holy water were followed by the destruction of the ouija board, all of which psychologically eased the family. Lucy vowed to renounce all occult practices. With this, the Glastonbury case ended, with no further reports of paranormal activity.

What's the answer?

This seems to have been another complex poltergeist episode involving, in this case, a young teen. While it's tempting to pin the whole incident on Lucy, there may be more to it. The teen years are hardly a picnic, but Lucy didn't seem particularly disturbed or frustrated. Also, ouija boards and some other methods of divining (see glossary) are known to cause paranormal trouble by helping some users make unintended "psychic connections" to Earth forces or parallel universes that could manifest as ghost or poltergeist phenomena.

In Lucy's case, we see the common phenomenon of the "spirit guide." Whether you call them guardian spirits, guardian angels or some aspect of your own subconscious or superconscious, my advice is to beware. Certainly, the presence in one's life of such a manifestation in a positive way is a recognized experience in many religions and can be an occasion for spiritual growth. But any experienced spiritual father or mother will tell you that when the manifestation *starts telling you what to do* – via a ouija board or any other medium — especially if it's against your instincts or judgment — get rid of it!

Perhaps the New Testament has the best advice: "...do not trust every spirit...." (1 John 4:1)

Faces at the Window

5

The Poltergeist that Threatened a Neighborhood

An original version of this story appeared as "A Poltergeist that Broke the Rules" in the June 1986 issue of FATE magazine. Original elements are used here by permission of Llewellyn Worldwide, Ltd.

Faces at the Window

July 1975 brought to the scene a Connecticut poltergeist that shattered not only dishes, knickknacks and people's nerves but also many of the rules associated with this terrifying phenomenon, at least as those rules were understood then. Unlike almost all poltergeists, this one seemed to be attached to no particular individual and appeared to travel at will, threatening an entire neighborhood.

The neighborhood itself was a Bristol housing development that had gobbled up most of an old hilltop farm. All but a few of the houses were new, with other lots farther up the road still undeveloped. Where the road entered the development, a farm building had been turned into a private home long before the newer houses were built. Adjacent to this boxy, brown structure stood a dilapidated cottage in the process of demolition.

Right across the road was the ranch house of John and Susan Sanford, both in their late 30s, and their two sons, aged 10 and 12. John Sanford, a real-estate agent, had helped sell the other neighborhood lots, and his house had been the first to be built, some three years earlier. Nothing particularly odd had disturbed the Sanfords during those years, but the most hellish month of their lives was about to begin that hot, mid-July week, apparently prompted by an act of kindness.

The Sanfords and their neighbors had long known that a middle-aged widow and her teenaged son lived in the old brown house across the road. No one knew them; they kept to themselves. When the boy, who was about 14, rode down the road on his bicycle, neighborhood children often taunted him, shouting, among other things, that his mother was a witch.

This upset Susan Sanford, so she decided to walk across the street and invite the mysterious neighbor to have coffee with her. Mrs. Sanford found a nervous but congenial 45-year-old woman whose name was Hobbes. Shortly, the two women were seated in the Sanford kitchen over coffee and

Faces at the Window

pastry. But the Sanfords' small dog, usually friendly, ran and hid as soon as Mrs. Hobbes entered the house, and he wouldn't come out until she left.

Unseen hands around his neck

It was a strange visit indeed, and the guest seemed reluctant to talk about herself. Mrs. Sanford had noticed that workmen who had been demolishing the old cottage adjacent to the Hobbes home had stopped. Asked why this was, Mrs. Hobbes casually related that, during the previous week, one of the workers had felt what he described as invisible "cold hands" around his neck and had fled the site, taking his crew with him. The men refused to return.

-Photo by Paul F. Eno

A disembodied face appears in the glassless window of this boarded-up door in the half-demolished shack near the Sanford home. At some of the author's lectures, some in the audience have screamed as soon as a slide of this photo appeared on the screen.

Faces at the Window

-Photo by Paul F. Eno

Two strange blobs of light appear on this photo, taken in the yard of the Hobbes home. Their house is at right.

The next day, Mrs. Hobbes returned the favor and invited her neighbor for tea. Mrs. Sanford found the Hobbes home gloomy and felt strangely uneasy there. She nearly choked on a sip of tea when an ash tray suddenly rose from the coffee table and floated across the room. Her hostess, not in the least surprised, declared, "Oh, that's only the ghost." Needless to say, Mrs. Sanford made a polite but hasty exit.

Mrs. Hobbes's next visit to the Sanford home, a few days later, was her last because, Mrs. Sanford later said, the woman "brought the thing with her."

The visit was pleasant enough, but paranormal activity erupted as soon as Mrs. Hobbes left. Dishes flew from their shelves and smashed on the floor. Furniture jumped around and pictures fell from the wall. Mrs. Sanford, understandably frantic, called her husband at his office and told him to come home. At about the same time, the two Sanford boys

Faces at the Window

got off the school bus at the corner. The activity had stopped by this time, but when the boys walked through the door, they thought the place had been broken into and ransacked. Before John Sanford saw the house for himself, he had thought his wife had been joking.

The Sanfords all felt that some unseen agency from across the street had been at work, and they believed that the old, half-demolished cottage had something to do with it.

Poltergeist phenomena plagued the Sanford home through the following week. Not only did objects move around by themselves, but all four family members heard an animal-like growling coming from beneath beds and other furniture. "Terrifying" eyes they described as "flaming red" appeared at windows, and knocks were heard at the doors at all hours of the day and night. Of course, when the doors were opened, no one was there.

Other homes affected

Toward the end of the week, the disturbances began to spread. The Sanfords learned that four neighboring families also had heard the strange knocks, and two of the neighbors had been frightened out of their wits by objects that moved by no apparent means.

Like many poltergeist victims, the Sanfords told no one what was happening for fear of ridicule. Only when a neighbor mentioned that strange things were happening at her house (on a more minor scale) did Mrs. Sanford learn the extent of the problem. Then she confided in her victimized neighbors.

An incident at the very end of the week shook the Sanfords into the realization that they needed help. In broad daylight, Mrs. Sanford saw a huge black form move through the field across the road and disappear into the wall of the old cottage. Not knowing what kind of help to get, the family confided in a friend who was a local radio personality. This man contacted me.

Faces at the Window

It was a grim, overcast day when I went to the Sanford house, where Mrs. Sanford and one of the affected neighbors filled me in on the most recent events. All phenomena seemed to have ceased, they said, after Mrs. Sanford saw the dark shape in the field.

A wall of electrical energy

After this initial briefing, I walked over to the Hobbes property to look at what was left of the cottage and to take photographs. Nothing unusual happened until I approached the structure. About 15 feet from the ruins, I was abruptly halted by what I can describe only as a wall of electrical energy. This phenomenon is familiar to investigators, but I had never encountered so strong a field. It engulfed the cottage and seemed equally strong at all points, so potent that my hair practically stood on end.

These feelings, along with the absence of high-tension wires or an impending electrical storm, led me to question my original suspicion that these people were the victims of a practical joker rather than a poltergeist. The site seemed to be a powerhouse of psychic energy.

When I returned to the Sanfords', I suggested that I talk to Mrs. Hobbes, her son and the other neighbors involved. I also wanted to return in a few days to go over the property again. With that I said good-bye and drove away. But, while I was willing to call it a day, whatever was plaguing the neighborhood wasn't. As I turned onto the main road, the same energy I had felt at the cottage became evident in my car. All at once, both doors flew open and a stiff wind tore through, blowing everything (except me, fortunately) out onto the road. My cars have never been known for interior neatness, so the debris I had to gather and stuff back inside was considerable. Feeling like a character in a horror movie, I made it home without further incident.

Two days later, I had a lab report confirming that what had appeared in two of my photographs couldn't be explained as ordinary photographic anomalies. In one, which graces the cover of this book, a bearded face seems to look out the bleary glass of a boarded-up window in the old cottage. In the other, two odd, bluish shapes seem to be taking form in the yard of the Hobbes house. Several associates of mine thought they saw the crouching figure of a stout little boy looking into a puddle before the ruins in a third photo, but a lab examination proved nothing.

News of 'Jeremy'

The next evening I went to a social gathering that included several psychics and investigators of the paranormal, some of whom knew about the Sanfords' poltergeist. Among the psychics was my friend Mary Pascarella, head of the Psychic Research Institute in Hamden, Connecticut, who sat down and told me what she thought was going on. I had given her some cursory information, and only later did she see the photographs.

Mary felt that a retarded child named Jeremy had been confined to the cottage in the late 19th or early 20th centuries. At that time, such children were considered a shame rather than an occasion for extra love. Many were locked away by their families and otherwise abused. This was the case with Jeremy, who was probably illegitimate, she said. She added that he was apparently "earthbound" in the old cottage where he had suffered so much torment. Naturally, the photo with the boy-like shape near the puddle came to mind.

When I told her what had happened in my car on the way home, Mary said the boy had followed me because he sensed I would understand him. (She knew I had worked with retarded children in the past.)

In theory, I was skeptical about the notion of earthbound spirits and preferred a more conventional explanation. But, as things turned out, we never got a chance to find out who was right.

All this time, my comrade in research, Louis Letendre, had been burrowing through Bristol town records. He found no mention of a "Jeremy," but this isn't surprising if he had been the kind of child Mary described. But Louis did find that the old cottage had a questionable reputation indeed: It had been the site of prostitution, bootlegging and other illegal activities during the 1920s.

A week after my initial interview with Susan Sanford, Louis and I were still trying to start an investigation. With overt phenomena having ceased, it proved difficult to get the Sanfords or their neighbors to cooperate further, even though they still felt they were in danger. Their primary reason was fear of the press, not hard to understand in view of the internationally publicized Bridgeport poltergeist case I had been involved with less than a year before. It proved just as difficult to contact Mrs. Hobbes; I never even saw her.

While we heard later that the phenomena had resumed for a brief period at the Sanfords', I was never again contacted for assistance. My radio newscaster friend said that the personalities of John and Susan Sanford had suddenly changed drastically, that the family's finances had collapsed and that divorce had been mentioned, all within a few months of the phenomena. Later, we heard that the family had moved away. We never found out whether the neighbors had any more trouble.

What's the answer?

While the Bristol case never resulted in a full investigation, I did have a brush with a very unusual poltergeist. And if I'd known then what I know now, I would have brought in electromagnetometers and other gizmos to measure Earth energies in the area. In those days, however, a paranormal investigation was very much a seat-of-the-pants operation.

I think we must look to the apparently troubled marriage

Faces at the Window

of John and Susan Sanford, coupled with an extremely powerful psychic residue in the old cottage and local Earth energies conducive to paranormal activity. Mix all this with the Hobbes's introverted personalities, then toss in a few extra-dimensional entities looking for a psychic "meal," and the "chemistry" would be just right for the kind of paranormal pyrotechnics the Sanfords and their neighbors described.

For whatever reason, John Sanford seemed to have had a great deal of repressed anger and resentment. His wife, though obviously intelligent and capable, seemed to be in a world of her own, harboring a certain amount of repressed emotion. But the two Sanford boys, of ages often associated with poltergeist phenomena, seemed well balanced and close to each other.

The later explosion of the Sanfords' repressed feelings, perhaps brought about by the reported financial troubles, may have been what lit the fuse. The phenomena apparently ran their course, as they usually do, then ended. As for Mrs. Hobbes and her son, they later moved away, and the cottage was torn down without further mishap.

When the personalities whose energies apparently fed it were gone, this unusually fierce neighborhood poltergeist certainly seems to have dissipated.

Whether my diagnosis is correct or whether "Jeremy" still broods in some parallel universe, awaiting the understanding he never had in one life or another, we probably will never know.

6

Into Thin Air: New England's Vanishing Ships

An original version of this story appeared as "New England's Vanishing Vessels" in the January and February 1987 issues of FATE magazine. Original elements are used here by permission of Llewellyn Worldwide, Ltd.

Faces at the Window

The Bermuda Triangle isn't the only place where ships vanish without a trace. New England has a venerable history of its own when it comes to mysterious disappearances, especially of ships and boats.

New England's coastal waters are dotted with commercial vessels of every description even in the winter. Around the clock, cargo vessels churn in and out of New England ports from New Haven, Connecticut, to Portland, Maine. In all but the worst weather, commercial fishing boats plow out of such smaller ports as Portsmouth, New Hampshire; Gloucester and New Bedford, Massachusetts; Galilee, Rhode Island, and Stonington, Connecticut. When the Gulf Stream and southerly winds waft summery weather our way, thousands of pleasure craft join the fray. Couple this with often bizarre weather conditions that can change almost instantly, and you have a recipe for the unexplained or the disastrous, or sometimes both.

In fact, a number of vessels seem to have ceased to exist in or near New England waters over the past 25 years. These include not only fishing boats and pleasure craft large and small but a 642-foot tanker carrying 2.2 million gallons of oil.

Through much of the 1980s, I was a public affairs officer in the U.S. Coast Guard Reserve, which put me in the perfect position not only to find out about such things but to have access to all the gory details. I spent many a weekend planted behind a desk in the Operations Center at the Coast Guard's First District headquarters in Boston "working" search and rescue cases as the press liaison. While I personally was involved with only one of the cases in this chapter (the *Sea Serpent* in 1985), I found all the others well documented in official – but unclassified — files.

It isn't all that easy for a vessel simply to evaporate. The Coast Guard is a crack military organization and its searches are extremely thorough. The service has a fast, efficient system on the local, national and international levels for dealing with rescue emergencies and missing craft. There is a three-tiered classification system for vessels whose whereabouts are unknown, depending on the length of time with no word: unreported, overdue and missing.

When it comes to search and rescue, not only are ships, aircraft and large numbers of personnel involved but so are advanced computers and other electronic gear. Local harbormasters, fishermen, boaters, police and fire departments are a regular part of all major searches. The Navy, Air Force, National Guard and foreign armed forces often pitch in.

Virtually instantaneous ship-to-shore radio communications make work and travel at sea much safer than they used to be. The Coast Guard constantly monitors radio traffic and knows immediately when someone is in trouble - if that someone has the few seconds necessary to tell it.

Despite all this, vessels seem to disappear in New England waters with disconcerting frequency, leaving little behind but official question marks and loved ones' pain.

The bizarre case of the 'Gulf Stream'

On a clear, crisp Saturday morning in January 1975, five men gathered on the dock behind Bigelow Laboratories in Boothbay Harbor, Maine. Laughing, joking and loaded with gear, they boarded the 54-foot research vessel *Gulf Stream* for a routine three-day mission: the recovery of eight oceanographic buoys in the Gulf of Maine. But these men never made their scheduled stop at Gloucester, Mass., that night because the *Gulf Stream* was sailing nowhere but into oblivion.

The Coast Guard and Navy launched a massive air and sea search that lasted a week and covered 77,000 square miles. But the *Gulf Stream* had vanished. An official inquiry into one of the strangest maritime disappearances on record yielded nothing but more questions.

"It's a mystery, that's all I can say," said Coast Guard

Lt. Michael Perkins, who headed the investigation.

The *Gulf Stream* was no ordinary vessel. Built in 1963 as a crew boat to service oil rigs in the Gulf of Mexico, she was a tough, steel-hulled craft thought to be more than able to handle anything reported in New England waters that year. Owned by Nova University of Fort Lauderdale, Florida, the boat had just been overhauled. She carried five powerful radio transmitters that could have broadcast distress signals to every possible rescuer. Her safety gear, including two self-inflating life rafts, was completely up-to-date.

Nor was hers an ordinary crew. Three of the five men were former naval officers and one was an internationally known oceanographer. Four worked for Nova University and one for the Scripps Institute of Oceanography in California. All had sailed together on a number of similar *Gulf Stream* missions. Capt. William B. Campbell was known as a capable, no-nonsense skipper who always was where he said he would be when he said he would be there.

Aside from the disappearance itself, the oddest thing about the case was what appeared to be the vessel's inexplicable behavior after leaving Boothbay Harbor.

Departing the Bigelow dock on Saturday, January 4, the *Gulf Stream* made a routine radio check, rounded McKown Point into the harbor, then headed southward and out to sea to retrieve a runaway buoy 77 miles southeast of Cape Cod. She was scheduled to come partway back that night and dock in Gloucester, go back out for more local buoy work Sunday, then return to Boothbay Harbor on Monday.

At about 10 p.m. Sunday, Petty Officer Leland Bugbee, the radioman on watch at Coast Guard Base South Portland, Maine, picked up the beginning of a transmission from the *Gulf Stream* but it was cut off in mid-sentence.

"A unit called," Bugbee reported. "We asked if it needed assistance and it came back and said, 'Coast Guard South Portland, this is *Gulf* -' "Bugbee noted that the voice "had that overtone of nervousness. You can't really explain it."

He said he tried for an hour and a half to reestablish contact but couldn't. The boat was never reported in port again, although Bigelow officials said she would have had to refuel Saturday night.

In one of the most peculiar incidents of the whole affair, two lobstermen familiar with the vessel's comings and goings later testified that they saw the *Gulf Stream* on Monday, January 6, the day she was supposed to return to Boothbay Harbor. Dicky and Paula Hammond were hauling lobster pots off Southport Island, just outside Boothbay Harbor, that morning and saw the *Gulf Stream* pass between them and Squirrel Island, about 500 yards away. The vessel was leaving the harbor, roaring off toward the south and out to sea just as if it were the previous Saturday.

At the subsequent Coast Guard inquiry, Hammond insisted that it was the *Gulf Stream* he saw.

"Particularly at this time of year, there's nothing around here that even looks like it," he said.

Not far away, another lobsterman, Wilson Francis, also was hauling traps. He said that he saw the *Gulf Stream* at the same time, although he hadn't noticed the name on her transom.

Both men thought there was nothing odd about this until they heard of the boat's disappearance - and of its departure on Saturday, not Monday.

That afternoon, retired Navy Comdr. William D. Howard, who had installed a new Motorola FM radio on the *Gulf Stream* the previous October, had his own radio on and heard a call from the boat.

"I recognized [Capt.] Campbell's voice.... It was very calm, answering or finishing a conversation," Howard said. "He wasn't calling anyone repeatedly, which I would have noticed."

The *Gulf Stream's* radios all had been in good shape when he had seen them in October, Howard said, noting that the

Faces at the Window

one he had installed was within arm's reach of the wheel, required no warm-up time and was automatically tuned to channel 16, the Coast Guard's emergency frequency. The *Gulf Stream* could have summoned help literally within seconds.

On Tuesday, the radioman at Coast Guard Station Point Allerton, at Hull, Massachusetts, thought he heard the *Gulf Stream* trying to contact Bigelow Laboratories. Also on Tuesday, a fishing boat heard the *Gulf Stream* trying to raise the Camden, Maine, marine operator. A Coast Guardsman who overheard this call described it as "normal" and "calm."

Another Coast Guardsman, this time at the Halfway Rock Light Station on Massachusetts's North Shore, said he heard the boat attempting to answer a call from Bigelow. That happened at about 2 p.m. — and it was the last anyone ever heard of the *Gulf Stream.*

Meanwhile, no one at Bigelow had heard anything from the vessel since it left Boothbay Harbor. So, late Tuesday, people there notified the Coast Guard that the *Gulf Stream* was overdue. This prompted the enormous search that grew to include three large Coast Guard cutters, numerous aircraft and small vessels from as far away as Virginia, the Navy and even another civilian research vessel. The Woods Hole Oceanographic Institution, Nova University and the Massachusetts Institute of Technology all lent technical help of one sort or another to try to figure out where the *Gulf Stream* could be.

The search itself scoured the coast from New Jersey to Nova Scotia and up to 300 miles out into the Atlantic. On Wednesday, January 8, the day after the *Gulf Stream* was reported overdue, the weather started getting nasty, and most of the aircraft were grounded.

Nothing at all turned up until that day, when a Coast Guard helicopter found a life ring from the *Gulf Stream* about 27 miles northeast of Gloucester. On Thursday, with the weather deteriorating, the 270-foot cutter *Duane* recovered the body of research technician James Riddle, wearing a life jacket, some 15 miles southwest of the same spot. A report later said he had died of exposure. Two more life rings were found 15 miles northeast of Gloucester on Friday.

By Monday, January 13, searchers were no closer to an answer than they had been when they started. Some bits of debris had been recovered, but these couldn't be traced to the *Gulf Stream*. The only other items that could be traced were a life jacket marked *Heldo*, the *Gulf Stream's* former name, and a drawer from a desk in the boat's innermost cabin. An airplane crew reported sighting what looked like a small oil slick and what might have been a deflated life raft, but these couldn't be located by surface craft.

A Coast Guard board of inquiry released its report in May. The panel was stumped not only by the apparently senseless behavior of the vessel but by the lack of an actual wreck or the debris from one.

Why did the cabin drawer end up floating away when the large stock of gear stowed on deck, including a 500-foot length of thick, floating plastic line, has never been found? Why was there no identifiable oil slick? What happened to the rest of the crew?

"We turned the Gulf of Maine upside down and wrung it out," one Coast Guard officer said. "They're not out there."

The board concluded that "due to the lack of any eyewitnesses, the proximate cause of the casualty cannot be determined at this time." They speculated that inclement weather on January 7 and lack of a firm sailing plan may have contributed to some sort of accident.

All we know for certain is that the *Gulf Stream* entered the shadows as one of New England's most baffling mysteries of the sea.

The vanishment
that troubled the White House

Certainly one of the most publicized disappearances in

recent times was that of the 60-foot offshore lobster boat *Zubenelgenubi.* Before the massive and controversial search ended, the president of the United States, the governor of Massachusetts, members of Congress and the commandant of the Coast Guard all got pulled in.

Two major storms struck while the *Zubenelgenubi* was presumably at sea, with winds up to 60 mph and seas as high as 35 feet. These things considered, its disappearance might not seem all that mysterious. But then again, the Newport, Rhode Island, vessel was big, brand-new and credited by those who knew it as being unsinkable, with a steel hull divided into four watertight bulkheads. She was considered one of the finest, safest vessels in the Newport fishing fleet.

Zubenelgenubi, named for the brightest star in the constellation Libra, left port with a crew of four on Sunday, January 18, 1976. It was to be a 10- to 14-day trip to tend lobster traps some 80 miles south of Nantucket, on the edge of the continental shelf.

A fisherman reported the last sighting of the vessel on Tuesday, January 20, when it evidently was *en route* to its fishing grounds. One week later, on January 27, a crewman's wife called the Coast Guard to say the *Zubenelgenubi* was unreported, but because the captain's wife didn't consider the vessel overdue, no search was ordered.

Coast Guard Station Brant Point, at the eastern end of Nantucket, reported what sounded like a routine conversation between the boat and a passing tanker on Friday, January 30. And three days later, on February 2, another fishing boat picked up what its captain thought was a transmission from the *Zubenelgenubi* reporting its position as Hydrographer Canyon, about 80 miles southeast of Nantucket. This was just before one of the storms struck. The captain's wife, Joanne Goodwin, reported the boat overdue the next day.

During a six-day search that combed 66,000 square miles and involved the Coast Guard, the Navy and the Canadian Armed Forces, absolutely nothing was found. The only possible clue was oil bubbling up to the surface at a point some 50 miles south of Nantucket, in water 500 feet deep. The cutter *Dallas* was asked to stop and take samples of the oil if it was passing the spot, which it never did. The oil never was tested but there was official speculation that it came from an old sunken tanker known to be at or near that spot. Coast Guard officials said that any connection with the *Zubenelgenubi* was dubious. Anyway, they added, it would take a submarine to find out.

The crew's families and friends refused to abandon hope after the official search was suspended on Sunday, February 8. A massive petition drive and a special town meeting in Marblehead, Massachusetts, Capt. Goodwin's hometown, prompted Sen. Edward Kennedy, Congressman Michael Harrington, Massachusetts Gov. Michael S. Dukakis and then-Lt. Gov. Thomas P. O'Neill (son of his namesake, the speaker of the U.S. House of Representatives) to lean on the Coast Guard to have the search resumed. Admiral William P. Siler, commandant of the Coast Guard, refused, saying that everything possible already had been done.

But other New England lawmakers joined the crusade, and the political temperature got too high. On February 12, President Gerald R. Ford personally ordered the Coast Guard to reopen the case for 24 hours. Once again, nothing was found. Efforts by those who believed the *Zubenelgenubi* crew was still alive continued and so did criticisms of the Coast Guard for allegedly searching in the wrong places and not being careful enough.

No sign of the vessel or its crew ever turned up, although the total search area reached 106,000 square miles before officials finally gave up.

A tanker disappears

On or about New Year's Day 1977, only a few days after the hair-raising breakup of the tanker *Argo Merchant* made global headlines in the heavy seas off Nantucket, the 642-foot tanker *Grand Zenith* disappeared off Nova Scotia. The ship had left England on December 19 bound for Providence, Rhode Island, carrying 2.2 million gallons of oil.

The *Grand Zenith* was last heard from on December 30 when she was in the middle of a winter storm some 230 miles east of Boston and about 60 miles south of Yarmouth, Nova Scotia. Her transmission was routine and gave no indication of trouble. When the tanker didn't arrive in Providence as scheduled on Sunday, January 2, the ship's agents reported her overdue.

Along with concern for the 38-member crew, officials were understandably terrified that another horrendous oil spill in the North Atlantic could threaten not only the shoreline but the vital fishing grounds at Georges and Browns Banks.

On January 3 and 4 Coast Guard and Canadian Forces units combed an area of 34,000 square miles along and near the ship's scheduled route from Nova Scotia to Narragansett Bay. They found no trace of the vessel. On January 5 the search was expanded to cover an area of about 100,000 square miles.

The cutter *Dallas* found a trace of oil on January 6, about 300 miles east of Cape Cod and 240 miles south of Halifax, Nova Scotia. Units also found two life jackets from the ship in the same area, along with a few pieces of flotsam. The oil was tested and it was believed to have come from the *Grand Zenith.*

Officials were astounded that these were the only traces of such a huge vessel. The subsequent investigation concluded that the *Grand Zenith* had somehow broken up in heavy seas during the storm. Officials were understandably mystified about the lack of a distress call, not to mention the fate of the oil, the crew and the ship.

The 378-foot, high-endurance USCGC Dallas often is involved in search-and-rescue operations off the East Coast of the United States. In the case of the **Grand Zenith,** *the* **Zubenelgenubi** *and a few others, the searches were fruitless.*

A gruesome catch

At about 8 a.m. on Sunday, January 8, 1978, the nets of the Italian fishing trawler *Corrado Secundo* made a gruesome catch 90 miles south of Martha's Vinyard, Massachusetts. It was the body of 31-year-old Richard Neild, who had disappeared a month before with the New Bedford, Massachusetts, scalloper *Navigator* and 12 other crewmen. A week-long search covering 104,000 square miles had revealed no trace of the 86-foot vessel or its crew.

The oddest thing about the find was the unconfirmed report that, under the usual oilskins worn by fishermen while at work, the body was clothed in a business suit.

The Navigator left New Bedford on November 30, 1977, for what was to be a scalloping trip to an area about 60 miles south of Nantucket. She was never seen again. The last confirmed contact with the vessel was that night, when the *Navigator's* captain, Norman A. Lepire, spoke by radio with his counterpart aboard another New Bedford scalloper, the *Oceanic.* Four other New Bedford vessels were fishing in the same area south of Nantucket during this whole period, but no one reported even a radio contact with the doomed ship.

Faces at the Window

The Navigator was a wooden-hulled vessel built in 1964. She carried three radios, two radar units, two Loran A navigation outfits, two fathometers and a magnetic compass. Local firms that serviced this equipment regularly told the Coast Guard that all systems were in good working order. Two weeks before her final voyage, the *Navigator* had spent five days being overhauled at the Norlantic boatyard in Fairhaven, Massachusetts.

The weather was good when the *Navigator* left New Bedford but got worse the next day as low pressure moved in. By December 6 winds were gusting to 40 knots.

The *Navigator's* owner, Myron D. Marder, reported her overdue on December 10. Lights burned late in the homes of the 13 crewmen, and special prayer services were held at New Bedford's historic Seaman's Bethel chapel, the same one mentioned in Herman Melville's *Moby Dick.*

The extensive search revealed no trace of the vessel. A Coast Guard inquiry concluded that she must have sunk but that "due to a lack of any distress signals, witnesses, survivors or positive, identifiable wreckage, the exact cause and nature of the casualty remains unknown." Poor weather may have been at least partially responsible, the report noted.

The Navigator tragedy was believed to be the worst loss of life in modern times for the New Bedford fishing community, one of the largest fleets in the nation.

The Captain Cosmo *tragedy*

That September the Massachusetts fishing port of Gloucester faced a tragedy of its own. Sometime after it left port on Saturday, September 2, 1978, the 86-foot trawler *Captain Cosmo* and her crew of six disappeared somewhere east of Cape Cod.

The ship was due to return to Gloucester on September 9 and was in radio contact with the fishing boat *St. Nicholas* on the 5th, 6th, and 7th when the *Captain Cosmo* was about 180 miles east of her home port. At that time, Capt. Cosmo

-Courtesy Boston Globe

The Gloucester, Massachusetts, fishing vessel Capt. Cosmo

Marcantonio told the *St. Nicholas* by radio that he was going to stay in that area to fish, then would head home and arrive there on schedule.

The fishing vessel *Madonna Delle Grazie* reported a radio conversation with the *Captain Cosmo* on September 9. The vessel reportedly was riding out high winds and 20-foot seas that struck the fishing grounds that day. That was the last anyone ever heard from the *Captain Cosmo*.

Faces at the Window

After an eight-day search that scoured 121,000 square miles, there was still no trace of the *Captain Cosmo* or her crew. The only shred of evidence about the vessel's fate came from a high-altitude photograph taken by an Air Force U-2 spy plane brought in from California especially for the search.

The photo, taken on September 14, was partially obscured by clouds. But it showed what could have been a vessel from 80 to 100 feet long lying just below the surface 250 miles east of Cape Cod. An intensive surface search found nothing.

The mystery of the Sea Mist

In November 1982 the 110-foot fishing vessel *Sea Mist* disappeared without a trace in an area 50 miles east of Cape Cod. Ironically, the *Sea Mist* was a former Coast Guard vessel: a World War II-vintage submarine chaser that civilians had purchased and turned into a trawler.

The *Sea Mist's* home port was in Virginia but she had been operating out of Boston, usually working the Franklin Swell area of the Georges Bank fishing grounds where she eventually was to vanish. On November 9 she left Boston with two people on board for a four- to six-day trip. The weather was excellent throughout the scheduled period of the trip but began to deteriorate about halfway through the ensuing search.

The captain's wife, Mrs. Thomas J. Kelly of Amesbury, Massachusetts, reported the *Sea Mist* overdue on the 16th. Her husband had 20 years' sailing experience and was equipped with the best modern safety and survival gear.

A confirmed sighting by another fishing vessel placed the *Sea Mist* at Franklin Swell on the ninth, and an unconfirmed report said she was there the next day as well. From November 16 to 21 the search was widened, covering 70,000 square miles. As in so many other cases, these efforts brought zero results.

Faces at the Window

The Sea Serpent

Shane Kemper and Marc Cram left Plymouth, Massachusetts, on March 6, 1985, for a one-day fishing trip to a point just off Provincetown, at the tip of Cape Cod. They were never seen again.

Three days later a hatch cover identified by Cram's father as being from their 32-foot fishing boat *Sea Serpent* was found on a beach near Plymouth. With the exception of a few other oddments found washed up along Cape Cod's shore over the next few weeks, no other trace of the boat or the young men was ever found. Divers checked possible wrecks in the area but found nothing related to the vanished boat.

Unlike most of the other losses we've examined, the *Sea Serpent* wasn't far from shore and disappeared in an area frequented by pleasure and commercial craft even in March.

What's the answer?

What happens to the vessels that vanish off New England is a question that frustrates and baffles the best minds at First Coast Guard District headquarters in Boston as well as leaders of the area's commercial fishing industry.

Three features are common to many of these cases. First, most disappearances occur among fishing boats, perhaps because they sail farther out, stay longer and see more bad weather than other craft. Second, all our cases took place in winter when the weather in New England waters is notoriously stormy. Last, many occurred in or near the fishing grounds east of Cape Cod, where weather conditions are particularly quirky, although less worthy vessels than those we have discussed rode out the same storms unharmed.

Besides conventional bad weather, theories range from drug-related piracy and murder to highly localized freak sea conditions and huge rogue waves. Others have speculated that currents carry the evidence away before searchers arrive, although it's hard to believe that any current could

Faces at the Window

94

move quickly enough to outrace aircraft covering tens of thousands of square miles in a few days. Unreported collisions with freighters always are a possibility, but this would make the absence of debris even harder to understand. Of course, there could be paranormal explanations, but authoritative speculation on that would be even more unlikely.

But why were there no survivors, few if any bodies, no distress calls and little or no traceable debris?

One possible explanation is piracy. To Americans who live in states that it can take days to drive across, New England may seem tiny. But our coastline, indented with many hundreds of harbors, inlets and coves, is thousands of miles long. From the first advent of the tax man in the mid 18th century, smugglers have reveled in stealing in and out of these sheltered, hard-to-monitor waterways.

During the War Between the States, the ease of slipping in and out of our coastal waters prompted the Confederacy to consider a far-fetched plan to invade Maine from the sea to open a second front.

In this century, rum-runners and "druggies" have been no strangers to this coast. The latter especially have been known to hijack boats, kill the crew, then repaint and renumber the vessels for use out of some faraway port.

Each week the Coast Guard in New England responds to many calls for help in life-threatening situations, some aboard fishing boats. Rarely is a life lost and, even after the worst (and quite infrequent) disasters, there is lots of oil, flotsam and other evidence of what happened. That's true except with the rare exceptions: the ones that just vanish.

In the end we are left only with the words of one frustrated Coast Guard officer: "The fact that nothing was heard... may indicate that [whatever happened] was so swift and complete that there was no time to send a Mayday."

Index

Faces at the Window

The author

PAUL F. ENO has been an investigator of paranormal phenomena for nearly 30 years. A prize-winning journalist who has done postgraduate work in psychology, philosophy, history, theology, literature and law, he has a special love for New England history and folklore. Mr. Eno is a former news editor at **The Providence Journal** *and a former managing editor of* **Observer Publications** *in Smithfield, R.I. Articles by him have appeared in* **Yankee, Fate, Pursuit, American History Illustrated,** *other national magazines in America and Britain and nearly every Rhode Island newspaper. Mr. Eno now works as a freelance writer, editor and publisher from his home in Woonsocket, R.I.*

Also by Paul F. Eno

(From New River Press, Woonsocket, R.I.)
The Best of Times (1992)
Underhill Days (1999)

(From Oxford University Press, London)
"William Blackstone"
in American National Biography

(From Pamphlet Publications, Chicago)
The Occult (1977)*
Preventive Medicine for the Occult
(1979)*

(coming from New River Press)
Footsteps in the Attic (2002)
Rhode Island: A Genial History (2003)

*out of print

Faces at the Window